S0-AHT-193

OPPOSING VIEWPOINTS® SERIES

Race in America

Other Books of Related Interest

Opposing Viewpoints Series

Culture Wars
Discrimination
Multiracial America
Reparations

At Issue Series

Interracial Relationships
Is Racism a Serious Problem?
Minorities and the Law
Racial Profiling

Current Controversies Series

Racial Profiling
Racism
Prisons
Rap Music and Culture

"Congress shall make no law ... abridging the freedom of speech, or of the press."

First Amendment to the US Constitution

The basic foundation of our democracy is the First Amendment guarantee of freedom of expression. The Opposing Viewpoints series is dedicated to the concept of this basic freedom and the idea that it is more important to practice it than to enshrine it.

Race in America

Susan Henneberg, Book Editor

GREENHAVEN PUBLISHING

Published in 2017 by Greenhaven Publishing, LLC
353 3rd Avenue, Suite 255, New York, NY 10010

Articles in Greenhaven Publishing anthologies are often edited for length to meet page
requirements. In addition, original titles of these works are changed to clearly present
the main thesis and to explicitly indicate the author's opinion. Every effort is made to
ensure that Greenhaven Publishing accurately reflects the original intent of the authors.
Every effort has been made to trace the owners of the copyrighted material.

Cover image:Lukas Maverick Greyson/Shutterstock.com

Library of Congress Cataloging-in-Publication Data

Names: Henneberg, Susan.
Title: Race in America / Susan Henneberg.
Description: New York : Greenhaven Publishing, 2017. |
Series: Opposing viewpoints | Includes index.
Identifiers: LCCN ISBN 9781534500280 (pbk.) | ISBN 9781534500228 (library bound)
Subjects: LCSH: United States—Race relations—Juvenile literature.
Classification: LCC E184.A1 H46 2017 | DDC 305.800973—dc23

Manufactured in the United States of America

Website: http://greenhavenpublishing.com

Contents

The Importance of Opposing Viewpoints

Perhaps every generation experiences a period in time in which the populace seems especially polarized, starkly divided on the important issues of the day and gravitating toward the far ends of the political spectrum and away from a consensus-facilitating middle ground. The world that today's students are growing up in and that they will soon enter into as active and engaged citizens is deeply fragmented in just this way. Issues relating to terrorism, immigration, women's rights, minority rights, race relations, health care, taxation, wealth and poverty, the environment, policing, military intervention, the proper role of government—in some ways, perennial issues that are freshly and uniquely urgent and vital with each new generation—are currently roiling the world.

If we are to foster a knowledgeable, responsible, active, and engaged citizenry among today's youth, we must provide them with the intellectual, interpretive, and critical-thinking tools and experience necessary to make sense of the world around them and of the all-important debates and arguments that inform it. After all, the outcome of these debates will in large measure determine the future course, prospects, and outcomes of the world and its peoples, particularly its youth. If they are to become successful members of society and productive and informed citizens, students need to learn how to evaluate the strengths and weaknesses of someone else's arguments, how to sift fact from opinion and fallacy, and how to test the relative merits and validity of their own opinions against the known facts and the best possible available information. The landmark series Opposing Viewpoints has been providing students with just such critical-thinking skills and exposure to the debates surrounding society's most urgent contemporary issues for many years, and it continues to serve this essential role with undiminished commitment, care, and rigor.

The key to the series's success in achieving its goal of sharpening students' critical-thinking and analytic skills resides in its title—

Opposing Viewpoints. In every intriguing, compelling, and engaging volume of this series, readers are presented with the widest possible spectrum of distinct viewpoints, expert opinions, and informed argumentation and commentary, supplied by some of today's leading academics, thinkers, analysts, politicians, policy makers, economists, activists, change agents, and advocates. Every opinion and argument anthologized here is presented objectively and accorded respect. There is no editorializing in any introductory text or in the arrangement and order of the pieces. No piece is included as a "straw man," an easy ideological target for cheap point-scoring. As wide and inclusive a range of viewpoints as possible is offered, with no privileging of one particular political ideology or cultural perspective over another. It is left to each individual reader to evaluate the relative merits of each argument— as he or she sees it, and with the use of ever-growing critical-thinking skills—and grapple with his or her own assumptions, beliefs, and perspectives to determine how convincing or successful any given argument is and how the reader's own stance on the issue may be modified or altered in response to it.

This process is facilitated and supported by volume, chapter, and selection introductions that provide readers with the essential context they need to begin engaging with the spotlighted issues, with the debates surrounding them, and with their own perhaps shifting or nascent opinions on them. In addition, guided reading and discussion questions encourage readers to determine the authors' point of view and purpose, interrogate and analyze the various arguments and their rhetoric and structure, evaluate the arguments' strengths and weaknesses, test their claims against available facts and evidence, judge the validity of the reasoning, and bring into clearer, sharper focus the reader's own beliefs and conclusions and how they may differ from or align with those in the collection or those of their classmates.

Research has shown that reading comprehension skills improve dramatically when students are provided with compelling, intriguing, and relevant "discussable" texts. The subject matter of these collections could not be more compelling, intriguing, or urgently relevant to today's students and the world they are poised to inherit. The anthologized articles and the reading and discussion questions that are included with them also provide the basis for stimulating, lively, and passionate classroom debates. Students who are compelled to anticipate objections to their own argument and identify the flaws in those of an opponent read more carefully, think more critically, and steep themselves in relevant context, facts, and information more thoroughly. In short, using discussable text of the kind provided by every single volume in the Opposing Viewpoints series encourages close reading, facilitates reading comprehension, fosters research, strengthens critical thinking, and greatly enlivens and energizes classroom discussion and participation. The entire learning process is deepened, extended, and strengthened.

For all of these reasons, Opposing Viewpoints continues to be exactly the right resource at exactly the right time—when we most need to provide readers with the critical-thinking tools and skills that will not only serve them well in school but also in their careers and their daily lives as decision-making family members, community members, and citizens. This series encourages respectful engagement with and analysis of opposing viewpoints and fosters a resulting increase in the strength and rigor of one's own opinions and stances. As such, it helps make readers "future ready," and that readiness will pay rich dividends for the readers themselves, for the citizenry, for our society, and for the world at large.

Introduction

> *"I'm here to say we must reject such despair. I'm here to insist that we are not as divided as we seem, and I know that because I know America. I know how far we've come against impossible odds."*
>
> —*Barack Obama, speaking at the memorial service for fallen Dallas police officers, July 12, 2016*

In 2008, while campaigning for president of the United States, then-Illinois Senator Barack Obama gave a speech about race in America. The speech, in part, was a response to incendiary sermons made by Obama's pastor, the Reverend Jeremiah Wright. Many Americans had been shocked by Wright's angry comments about the government, race relations, Jews, and the terrorist attacks on 9/11. While Obama denounced Wright's remarks, he did not renounce his relationship with his pastor, at least not then. Instead, he used the controversy as an opportunity to address the issue of race relations in the speech entitled "A More Perfect Union." Moving toward a post-race society, he said, means solving the problems that cause racism, such as poverty and lack of opportunity.

The fact is that the comments that have been made and the issues that have surfaced over the last few weeks reflect the complexities of race in this country that we've never really worked through—a part of our union that we have yet to perfect. And if we walk away now, if we simply retreat into our respective corners, we will never be able to come together and solve challenges like health care, or education, or the need to find good jobs for every American.

Obama was generally optimistic about race relations in the United States. He reminded Americans about the legacy of slavery, Jim Crow, and discrimination with which the country had struggled since its beginning. He recognized the anger and frustration that Reverend Wright and other African Americans felt and that "may not always feel productive." But, he said, condemning the anger without understanding its source "only serves to widen the chasm of misunderstanding that exists between the races." Many Americans celebrated this speech as the beginning of a new era in race relations in the United States when that chasm would be narrowed. A year after Barack Obama was elected president, conservative radio host Lou Dobbs declared "We are now in a twentieth-first century post-partisan, post racial society." A *New York Times*/CBS News poll soon after the 2008 election showed that 66 percent of poll participants thought that race relations in the United States were generally good.

By the end of President Obama's second term, much of the optimism about race relations in the nation had faded. A 2016 *New York Times*/CBS news poll showed that 69 percent of Americans thought race relations were generally bad and getting worse. High profile cases of violence between law enforcement and black citizens captured headlines during this time. In July, 2014 Eric Garner, an African American man arrested for selling individual cigarettes, died after a police chokehold cut off his oxygen. In August 2014, Michael Brown, an eighteen-year-old African American, was shot by police after a confrontation on a city street. In November 2014, twelve-year-old Tamir Rice was shot in Cleveland, Ohio, while carrying a toy replica gun. In April 2014, Walter Scott, a South Carolina black man, was shot by a police officer after a traffic stop. Also that month, Freddie Gray, arrested, handcuffed, and placed in a police wagon unsecured by a seatbelt, suffered fatal injuries while being transported to jail.

During the last year of President Obama's second term in office, racial conflict seemed to be increasing. July 2016 was a difficult month for widely publicized police shootings. Alton Sterling , a black Baton Rouge, Louisiana, resident, was shot by police during an investigation for allegedly pointing a gun while selling CDs at a convenience store. The next day, Philando Castile, a black Minnesota driver, was shot during a traffic stop while reaching toward his back pants pocket. A few days later, during a Dallas rally to protest the killings, a black sniper shot at police, killing five. The following week, three Baton Rouge officers were fatally shot by a black ex-marine.

Statistics gathered by the Marshall Project, a news agency that tracks criminal justice in the United States, painted a grim picture of racial disparity in policing. According to the *Washington Post*, unarmed black men were seven times more likely than whites to die by police gunfire. It also reported that only a small percent of officers who were charged with felony manslaughter were convicted. Some of the fatal encounters between black citizens and police began with a low-level interaction such as a traffic stop. In 2015, CNN reported on the many cities that targeted low-income and minority residents with tickets and fines for minor offences. A 2011 Justice Department study found that a black driver is 31 percent more likely to be pulled over by law enforcement than a white driver. In 2016, South Carolina Senator Tim Scott, at that time one of two African Americans in the Senate, reported being stopped seven times in one year.

Again Obama gave a speech on race, this time at a memorial for the five police officers slain in Dallas in July of 2016. Referencing the violence during his last term in office, he said, "Faced with this violence, we wonder if the divides of race in America can ever be bridged." The following chapters ask some hard questions about race in America: *Are we living in a post-racial society? Is race overemphasized? Is justice color-blind? Can the United States overcome its history of racism?* After reading the articles, readers can draw their own conclusions about this vital topic.

OPPOSING VIEWPOINTS® SERIES

CHAPTER 1

Are We Living in a Post-Racial Society?

Chapter Preface

M any Americans were optimistic that the country was moving forward in race relations when they elected the first African American president in 2008. In the years since, much of that optimism has vanished. Polls show that Americans are concerned about the state of race relations and the increase in racial violence. A large percent of poll respondents expressed a need for changes in the country to achieve racial equality.

Among the changes many people think are needed are policies to address the large economic gap between black and white households. The Great Recession impacted the two groups unequally, and wealth inequality has widened along racial and ethnic lines. Minority families fall below white families in median income, home ownership, and educational achievement. White households are recovering from the recession at a faster rate than black households.

Some commentators compare the state of race relations today with the situation during the civil rights period of the 1960s. Racial violence then brought attention to the high levels of discrimination felt by black Americans, especially in the south. However, white political moderates in the rest of the country stepped up and passed the Civil Rights Acts of 1964. Currently, many black Americans feel as if those moderates are silent.

While open discrimination against racial minorities has been reduced since the civil rights era, many people in the black community express frustration at the more covert racism they experience as part of daily life. Being accused of using affirmative action to get positions in universities rather than earning their spot on merit or being frequent victims of traffic stops are common occurrences for many people of color. White Americans benefit from white privilege, black commentators say, while claiming that they are not part of any prejudicial group or community.

The debate continues about the impact of the first black presidency and whether the United States has achieved a post-race society. Readers can make up their own minds as they answer the question of whether the United States has achieved a society where race is not an impediment to success.

> "*In the white community, the path to a more perfect union means acknowledging that what ails the African-American community does not just exist in the minds of black people; that the legacy of discrimination—and current incidents of discrimination, while less overt than in the past—are real and must be addressed.*"

We Can Achieve a More Perfect Union

Barack Obama

Speaking before supporters at the National Constitution Center in Philadelphia, Pennsylvania, presidential candidate Barack Obama used terms from the Preamble to the Constitution to explain his vision of a post-racial America. He discussed racial tensions, white privilege, and inequality in the United States as a way of contextualizing the controversial statements by his former pastor, Reverend Jeremiah Wright. He asked the nation to move beyond a stalemate in race relations to address social problems common to all. Barack Obama is the forty-fourth president of the United States.

"Remarks of Senator Barack Obama: 'A More Perfect Union,'" Barack Obama, March 18, 2008.

As you read, consider the following questions:

1. How does Barack Obama's own story relate to the overall theme of the speech?
2. What are the conflicts involved with Obama's relationship with the Reverend Jeremiah Wright?
3. In what ways does Obama believe that discrimination against African Americans needs to be addressed?

W e the people, in order to form a more perfect union."
Two hundred and twenty one years ago, in a hall that still stands across the street, a group of men gathered and, with these simple words, launched America's improbable experiment in democracy. Farmers and scholars; statesmen and patriots who had traveled across an ocean to escape tyranny and persecution finally made real their declaration of independence at a Philadelphia convention that lasted through the spring of 1787.

The document they produced was eventually signed but ultimately unfinished. It was stained by this nation's original sin of slavery, a question that divided the colonies and brought the convention to a stalemate until the founders chose to allow the slave trade to continue for at least twenty more years, and to leave any final resolution to future generations.

Of course, the answer to the slavery question was already embedded within our Constitution—a Constitution that had at its very core the ideal of equal citizenship under the law; a Constitution that promised its people liberty, and justice, and a union that could be and should be perfected over time.

And yet words on a parchment would not be enough to deliver slaves from bondage, or provide men and women of every color and creed their full rights and obligations as citizens of the United States. What would be needed were Americans in successive generations who were willing to do their part—through protests and struggle, on the streets and in the courts, through a civil war and civil disobedience and always at great risk—to narrow that gap between the promise of our ideals and the reality of their time.

This was one of the tasks we set forth at the beginning of this campaign—to continue the long march of those who came before us, a march for a more just, more equal, more free, more caring and more prosperous America. I chose to run for the presidency at this moment in history because I believe deeply that we cannot solve the challenges of our time unless we solve them together—unless we perfect our union by understanding that we may have different stories, but we hold common hopes; that we may not look the same and we may not have come from the same place, but we all want to move in the same direction—towards a better future for our children and our grandchildren.

This belief comes from my unyielding faith in the decency and generosity of the American people. But it also comes from my own American story.

I am the son of a black man from Kenya and a white woman from Kansas. I was raised with the help of a white grandfather who survived a Depression to serve in Patton's Army during World War II and a white grandmother who worked on a bomber assembly line at Fort Leavenworth while he was overseas. I've gone to some of the best schools in America and lived in one of the world's poorest nations. I am married to a black American who carries within her the blood of slaves and slaveowners—an inheritance we pass on to our two precious daughters. I have brothers, sisters, nieces, nephews, uncles and cousins, of every race and every hue, scattered across three continents, and for as long as I live, I will never forget that in no other country on Earth is my story even possible.

It's a story that hasn't made me the most conventional candidate. But it is a story that has seared into my genetic makeup the idea that this nation is more than the sum of its parts—that out of many, we are truly one.

Throughout the first year of this campaign, against all predictions to the contrary, we saw how hungry the American people were for this message of unity. Despite the temptation to view my candidacy through a purely racial lens, we won commanding victories in states with some of the whitest populations in the country. In South Carolina, where the Confederate Flag still flies, we built a powerful coalition of African Americans and white Americans.

This is not to say that race has not been an issue in the campaign. At various stages in the campaign, some commentators have deemed me either "too black" or "not black enough." We saw racial tensions bubble to the surface during the week before the South Carolina primary. The press has scoured every exit poll for the latest evidence of racial polarization, not just in terms of white and black, but black and brown as well.

And yet, it has only been in the last couple of weeks that the discussion of race in this campaign has taken a particularly divisive turn.

On one end of the spectrum, we've heard the implication that my candidacy is somehow an exercise in affirmative action; that it's based solely on the desire of wide-eyed liberals to purchase racial reconciliation on the cheap. On the other end, we've heard my former pastor, Reverend Jeremiah Wright, use incendiary language to express views that have the potential not only to widen the racial divide, but views that denigrate both the greatness and the goodness of our nation; that rightly offend white and black alike.

I have already condemned, in unequivocal terms, the statements of Reverend Wright that have caused such controversy. For some, nagging questions remain. Did I know him to be an occasionally fierce critic of American domestic and foreign policy? Of course. Did I ever hear him make remarks that could be considered controversial while I sat in church? Yes. Did I strongly disagree with many of his political views? Absolutely—just as I'm sure many of you have heard remarks from your pastors, priests, or rabbis with which you strongly disagreed.

But the remarks that have caused this recent firestorm weren't simply controversial. They weren't simply a religious leader's effort to speak out against perceived injustice. Instead, they expressed a profoundly distorted view of this country—a view that sees white racism as endemic, and that elevates what is wrong with America above all that we know is right with America; a view that sees the conflicts in the Middle East as rooted primarily in the actions of stalwart allies like Israel, instead of emanating from the perverse and hateful ideologies of radical Islam.

As such, Reverend Wright's comments were not only wrong but divisive, divisive at a time when we need unity; racially charged at a time when we need to come together to solve a set of monumental problems—two wars, a terrorist threat, a falling economy, a chronic health care crisis and potentially devastating climate change; problems that are neither black or white or Latino or Asian, but rather problems that confront us all.

Given my background, my politics, and my professed values and ideals, there will no doubt be those for whom my statements of condemnation are not enough. Why associate myself with Reverend Wright in the first place, they may ask? Why not join another church? And I confess that if all that I knew of Reverend Wright were the snippets of those sermons that have run in an endless loop on the television and You Tube, or if Trinity United Church of Christ conformed to the caricatures being peddled by some commentators, there is no doubt that I would react in much the same way.

But the truth is, that isn't all that I know of the man. The man I met more than twenty years ago is a man who helped introduce me to my Christian faith, a man who spoke to me about our obligations to love one another; to care for the sick and lift up the poor. He is a man who served his country as a U.S. Marine; who has studied and lectured at some of the finest universities and seminaries in the country, and who for over thirty years led a church that serves the community by doing God's work here on Earth—by housing the homeless, ministering to the needy, providing day care services and scholarships and prison ministries, and reaching out to those suffering from HIV/AIDS.

In my first book, *Dreams From My Father*, I described the experience of my first service at Trinity:

People began to shout, to rise from their seats and clap and cry out, a forceful wind carrying the reverend's voice up into the rafters. … And in that single note—hope!—I heard something else; at the foot of that cross, inside the thousands of churches across the city, I imagined the stories of ordinary black people merging with the stories of David and Goliath, Moses and Pharaoh, the Christians in the lion's den, Ezekiel's field of dry bones. Those stories—of survival, and freedom, and hope— became our story, my story; the blood that had spilled was our blood, the tears our tears; until this black church, on this bright day, seemed once more a vessel carrying the story of a people into future generations and into a larger world. Our trials and triumphs became at once unique and universal, black and more than black; in chronicling our journey, the stories and songs gave us a means to reclaim memories that we didn't need to feel shame about … memories that all people might study and cherish—and with which we could start to rebuild.

That has been my experience at Trinity. Like other predominantly black churches across the country, Trinity embodies the black community in its entirety—the doctor and the welfare mom, the model student and the former gang-banger. Like other black churches, Trinity's services are full of raucous laughter and sometimes bawdy humor. They are full of dancing, clapping, screaming and shouting that may seem jarring to the untrained ear. The church contains in full the kindness and cruelty, the fierce intelligence and the shocking ignorance, the struggles and successes, the love and yes, the bitterness and bias that make up the black experience in America.

And this helps explain, perhaps, my relationship with Reverend Wright. As imperfect as he may be, he has been like family to me. He strengthened my faith, officiated my wedding, and baptized my children. Not once in my conversations with him have I heard him talk about any ethnic group in derogatory terms, or treat whites with whom he interacted with anything but courtesy and respect. He contains within him the contradictions—the good and the bad —of the community that he has served diligently for so many years.

I can no more disown him than I can disown the black community. I can no more disown him than I can my white grandmother—a woman who helped raise me, a woman who sacrificed again and again for me, a woman who loves me as much as she loves anything in this world, but a woman who once confessed her fear of black men who passed by her on the street, and who on more than one occasion has uttered racial or ethnic stereotypes that made me cringe.

These people are a part of me. And they are a part of America, this country that I love.

Some will see this as an attempt to justify or excuse comments that are simply inexcusable. I can assure you it is not. I suppose the politically safe thing would be to move on from this episode and just hope that it fades into the woodwork. We can dismiss Reverend Wright as a crank or a demagogue, just as some have dismissed Geraldine Ferraro, in the aftermath of her recent statements, as harboring some deep-seated racial bias.

But race is an issue that I believe this nation cannot afford to ignore right now. We would be making the same mistake that Reverend Wright made in his offending sermons about America— to simplify and stereotype and amplify the negative to the point that it distorts reality.

The fact is that the comments that have been made and the issues that have surfaced over the last few weeks reflect the complexities of race in this country that we've never really worked through—a part of our union that we have yet to perfect. And if we walk away now, if we simply retreat into our respective corners, we will never be able to come together and solve challenges like health care, or education, or the need to find good jobs for every American.

Understanding this reality requires a reminder of how we arrived at this point. As William Faulkner once wrote, "The past isn't dead and buried. In fact, it isn't even past." We do not need to recite here the history of racial injustice in this country. But we do need to remind ourselves that so many of the disparities that exist in the African-American community today can be directly traced to inequalities passed on from an earlier generation that suffered under the brutal legacy of slavery and Jim Crow.

Segregated schools were, and are, inferior schools; we still haven't fixed them, fifty years after *Brown v. Board of Education*, and the inferior education they provided, then and now, helps explain the pervasive achievement gap between today's black and white students.

Legalized discrimination—where blacks were prevented, often through violence, from owning property, or loans were not granted to African-American business owners, or black homeowners could not access FHA mortgages, or blacks were excluded from unions, or the police force, or fire departments—meant that black families could not amass any meaningful wealth to bequeath to future generations. That history helps explain the wealth and income gap between black and white, and the concentrated pockets of poverty that persists in so many of today's urban and rural communities.

A lack of economic opportunity among black men, and the shame and frustration that came from not being able to provide for one's family, contributed to the erosion of black families—a problem that welfare policies for many years may have worsened. And the lack of basic services in so many urban black neighborhoods— parks for kids to play in, police walking the beat, regular garbage pick-up and building code enforcement—all helped create a cycle of violence, blight and neglect that continue to haunt us.

This is the reality in which Reverend Wright and other African-Americans of his generation grew up. They came of age in the late fifties and early sixties, a time when segregation was still the law of the land and opportunity was systematically constricted. What's remarkable is not how many failed in the face of discrimination, but rather how many men and women overcame the odds; how many were able to make a way out of no way for those like me who would come after them.

But for all those who scratched and clawed their way to get a piece of the American Dream, there were many who didn't make it—those who were ultimately defeated, in one way or another, by discrimination. That legacy of defeat was passed on to future generations—those young men and increasingly young women who we see standing on street corners or languishing in our prisons, without hope or prospects for the future. Even for those blacks who did make it, questions of race, and racism, continue to define their worldview in fundamental ways. For the men and women of Reverend Wright's generation, the memories of humiliation and doubt and fear have not gone away; nor has the anger and the bitterness of those years. That anger may not get expressed in public, in front of white co-workers or white friends. But it does find voice in the barbershop or around the kitchen table. At times, that anger is exploited by politicians, to gin up votes along racial lines, or to make up for a politician's own failings.

And occasionally it finds voice in the church on Sunday morning, in the pulpit and in the pews. The fact that so many people are surprised to hear that anger in some of Reverend Wright's sermons simply reminds us of the old truism that the most segregated hour in American life occurs on Sunday morning. That anger is not always productive; indeed, all too often it distracts attention from solving real problems; it keeps us from squarely facing our own complicity in our condition, and prevents the African-American community from forging the alliances it needs to bring about real change. But the anger is real; it is powerful; and to simply wish it away, to condemn it without understanding its roots, only serves to widen the chasm of misunderstanding that exists between the races.

In fact, a similar anger exists within segments of the white community. Most working- and middle-class white Americans don't feel that they have been particularly privileged by their race. Their experience is the immigrant experience—as far as they're concerned, no one's handed them anything, they've built it from scratch. They've worked hard all their lives, many times only to see their jobs shipped overseas or their pension dumped after a lifetime of labor. They are anxious about their futures, and feel their dreams slipping away; in an era of stagnant wages and global competition, opportunity comes to be seen as a zero sum game, in which your dreams come at my expense. So when they are told to bus their children to a school across town; when they hear that an African American is getting an advantage in landing a good job or a spot in a good college because of an injustice that they themselves never committed; when they're told that their fears about crime in urban neighborhoods are somehow prejudiced, resentment builds over time.

Like the anger within the black community, these resentments aren't always expressed in polite company. But they have helped shape the political landscape for at least a generation. Anger over welfare and affirmative action helped forge the Reagan Coalition. Politicians routinely exploited fears of crime for their own electoral ends. Talk show hosts and conservative commentators built entire careers unmasking bogus claims of racism while dismissing legitimate discussions of racial injustice and inequality as mere political correctness or reverse racism.

Just as black anger often proved counterproductive, so have these white resentments distracted attention from the real culprits of the middle class squeeze—a corporate culture rife with inside dealing, questionable accounting practices, and short-term greed; a Washington dominated by lobbyists and special interests; economic policies that favor the few over the many. And yet, to wish away the resentments of white Americans, to label them as misguided or even racist, without recognizing they are grounded in legitimate concerns—this too widens the racial divide, and blocks the path to understanding.

This is where we are right now. It's a racial stalemate we've been stuck in for years. Contrary to the claims of some of my critics, black and white, I have never been so naïve as to believe that we can get beyond our racial divisions in a single election cycle, or with a single candidacy—particularly a candidacy as imperfect as my own.

But I have asserted a firm conviction—a conviction rooted in my faith in God and my faith in the American people—that working together we can move beyond some of our old racial wounds, and that in fact we have no choice if we are to continue on the path of a more perfect union.

For the African-American community, that path means embracing the burdens of our past without becoming victims of our past. It means continuing to insist on a full measure of justice in every aspect of American life. But it also means binding our particular grievances—for better health care, and better schools, and better jobs—to the larger aspirations of all Americans—the white woman struggling to break the glass ceiling, the white man whose been laid off, the immigrant trying to feed his family. And it means taking full responsibility for own lives—by demanding more from our fathers, and spending more time with our children, and reading to them, and teaching them that while they may face challenges and discrimination in their own lives, they must never succumb to despair or cynicism; they must always believe that they can write their own destiny.

Ironically, this quintessentially American—and yes, conservative—notion of self-help found frequent expression in Reverend Wright's sermons. But what my former pastor too often failed to understand is that embarking on a program of self-help also requires a belief that society can change.

The profound mistake of Reverend Wright's sermons is not that he spoke about racism in our society. It's that he spoke as if our society was static; as if no progress has been made; as if this country—a country that has made it possible for one of his own members to run for the highest office in the land and build a coalition of white and black; Latino and Asian, rich and poor, young and old—is still irrevocably bound to a tragic past. But what we know—what we have seen—is that America can change. That is the true genius of this nation. What we have already achieved gives us hope—the audacity to hope—for what we can and must achieve tomorrow.

In the white community, the path to a more perfect union means acknowledging that what ails the African-American community does not just exist in the minds of black people; that the legacy of discrimination—and current incidents of discrimination, while less overt than in the past—are real and must be addressed. Not just with words, but with deeds—by investing in our schools and our communities; by enforcing our civil rights laws and ensuring fairness in our criminal justice system; by providing this generation with ladders of opportunity that were unavailable for previous generations. It requires all Americans to realize that your dreams do not have to come at the expense of my dreams; that investing in the health, welfare, and education of black and brown and white children will ultimately help all of America prosper.

In the end, then, what is called for is nothing more, and nothing less, than what all the world's great religions demand—that we do unto others as we would have them do unto us. Let us be our brother's keeper, Scripture tells us. Let us be our sister's keeper. Let us find that common stake we all have in one another, and let our politics reflect that spirit as well.

For we have a choice in this country. We can accept a politics that breeds division, and conflict, and cynicism. We can tackle race only as spectacle—as we did in the OJ trial—or in the wake of tragedy, as we did in the aftermath of Katrina—or as fodder for the nightly news. We can play Reverend Wright's sermons on every channel, every day and talk about them from now until the election, and make the only question in this campaign whether or not the American people think that I somehow believe or sympathize with his most offensive words. We can pounce on some gaffe by a Hillary supporter as evidence that she's playing the race card, or we can speculate on whether white men will all flock to John McCain in the general election regardless of his policies.

We can do that.

But if we do, I can tell you that in the next election, we'll be talking about some other distraction. And then another one. And then another one. And nothing will change.

That is one option. Or, at this moment, in this election, we can come together and say, "Not this time." This time we want to talk about the crumbling schools that are stealing the future of black children and white children and Asian children and Hispanic children and Native American children. This time we want to reject the cynicism that tells us that these kids can't learn; that those kids who don't look like us are somebody else's problem. The children of America are not those kids, they are our kids, and we will not let them fall behind in a 21st century economy. Not this time.

This time we want to talk about how the lines in the Emergency Room are filled with whites and blacks and Hispanics who do not have health care; who don't have the power on their own to overcome the special interests in Washington, but who can take them on if we do it together.

This time we want to talk about the shuttered mills that once provided a decent life for men and women of every race, and the homes for sale that once belonged to Americans from every religion, every region, every walk of life. This time we want to talk about the fact that the real problem is not that someone who doesn't look like you might take your job; it's that the corporation you work for will ship it overseas for nothing more than a profit.

This time we want to talk about the men and women of every color and creed who serve together, and fight together, and bleed together under the same proud flag. We want to talk about how to bring them home from a war that never should've been authorized and never should've been waged, and we want to talk about how we'll show our patriotism by caring for them, and their families, and giving them the benefits they have earned.

I would not be running for President if I didn't believe with all my heart that this is what the vast majority of Americans want for this country. This union may never be perfect, but generation after generation has shown that it can always be perfected. And today, whenever I find myself feeling doubtful or cynical about this possibility, what gives me the most hope is the next generation—the young people whose attitudes and beliefs and openness to change have already made history in this election.

There is one story in particularly that I'd like to leave you with today—a story I told when I had the great honor of speaking on Dr. King's birthday at his home church, Ebenezer Baptist, in Atlanta.

There is a young, twenty-three year old white woman named Ashley Baia who organized for our campaign in Florence, South Carolina. She had been working to organize a mostly African-American community since the beginning of this campaign, and one day she was at a roundtable discussion where everyone went around telling their story and why they were there.

And Ashley said that when she was nine years old, her mother got cancer. And because she had to miss days of work, she was let go and lost her health care. They had to file for bankruptcy, and that's when Ashley decided that she had to do something to help her mom.

She knew that food was one of their most expensive costs, and so Ashley convinced her mother that what she really liked and really wanted to eat more than anything else was mustard and relish sandwiches. Because that was the cheapest way to eat.

She did this for a year until her mom got better, and she told everyone at the roundtable that the reason she joined our campaign was so that she could help the millions of other children in the country who want and need to help their parents too.

Now Ashley might have made a different choice. Perhaps somebody told her along the way that the source of her mother's problems were blacks who were on welfare and too lazy to work, or Hispanics who were coming into the country illegally. But she didn't. She sought out allies in her fight against injustice.

Anyway, Ashley finishes her story and then goes around the room and asks everyone else why they're supporting the campaign. They all have different stories and reasons. Many bring up a specific issue. And finally they come to this elderly black man who's been sitting there quietly the entire time. And Ashley asks him why he's there. And he does not bring up a specific issue. He does not say health care or the economy. He does not say education or the war. He does not say that he was there because of Barack Obama. He simply says to everyone in the room, "I am here because of Ashley."

"I'm here because of Ashley." By itself, that single moment of recognition between that young white girl and that old black man is not enough. It is not enough to give health care to the sick, or jobs to the jobless, or education to our children.

But it is where we start. It is where our union grows stronger. And as so many generations have come to realize over the course of the two-hundred and twenty one years since a band of patriots signed that document in Philadelphia, that is where the perfection begins.

> *"The wealth of white households was 13 times the median wealth of black households in 2013, compared with eight times the wealth in 2010, according to a new Pew Research Center analysis of data from the Federal Reserve's Survey of Consumer Finances."*

There Is a Significant Wealth Gap between Black and White Households

Rakesh Kochhar and Richard Fry

In the following viewpoint, the authors argue that wealth inequality has widened along racial and ethnic lines since the end of the Great Recession. In 2013, the gap between black and white households reached its highest point since 1989. White households were able to recover more quickly from the Great Recession because their median incomes were higher, their home ownership rates were higher, and they had other assets such as stocks and retirement accounts that African American families did not. Rakesh Kochhar is an associate director of research at Pew Research Center. Richard Fry is a senior researcher at Pew Research Center.

"Wealth Inequality Has Widened Along Racial, Ethnic Lines since the End of the Great Recession," Pew Research Center, Washington, DC (December, 2014). http://www.pewresearch.org/fact-tank/2014/12/12/racial-wealth-gaps-great-recession/. Reprinted by.permission.

As you read, consider the following questions:

1. What impact did the Great Recession have on the net worth of American families overall?
2. Why did the recession create a greater impact on minority households than white households?
3. Why were white households able to recover more quickly than minority households from the effects of the Great Recession?

The Great Recession, fueled by the crises in the housing and financial markets, was universally hard on the net worth of American families. But even as the economic recovery has begun to mend asset prices, not all households have benefited alike, and wealth inequality has widened along racial and ethnic lines.

The wealth of white households was 13 times the median wealth of black households in 2013, compared with eight times the wealth in 2010, according to a new Pew Research Center analysis of data from the Federal Reserve's Survey of Consumer Finances. Likewise, the wealth of white households is now more than 10 times the wealth of Hispanic households, compared with nine times the wealth in 2010.

The current gap between blacks and whites has reached its highest point since 1989, when whites had 17 times the wealth of black households. The current white-to-Hispanic wealth ratio has reached a level not seen since 2001. (Asians and other racial groups are not separately identified in the public-use versions of the Fed's survey.)

Leaving aside race and ethnicity, the net worth of American families overall—the difference between the values of their assets and liabilities—held steady during the economic recovery. The typical household had a net worth of $81,400 in 2013, according to the Fed's survey—almost the same as what it was in 2010, when the median net worth of U.S. households was $82,300 (values expressed in 2013 dollars).

The stability in household wealth follows a dramatic drop during the Great Recession. From 2007 to 2010, the median net worth of American families decreased by 39.4%, from $135,700 to $82,300. Rapidly plunging house prices and a stock market crash were the immediate contributors to this shellacking.

Our analysis of Federal Reserve data does reveal a stark divide in the experiences of white, black and Hispanic households during the economic recovery. From 2010 to 2013, the median wealth of non-Hispanic white households increased from $138,600 to $141,900, or by 2.4%.

Meanwhile, the median wealth of non-Hispanic black households fell 33.7%, from $16,600 in 2010 to $11,000 in 2013. Among Hispanics, median wealth decreased by 14.3%, from $16,000 to $13,700. For all families—white, black and Hispanic—median wealth is still less than its pre-recession level.

A number of factors seem responsible for the widening of the wealth gaps during the economic recovery. As the Federal Reserve notes, the median income of minority households (blacks, Hispanics and other non-whites combined) fell 9% from its 2010 to 2013 surveys, compared with a decrease of 1% for non-Hispanic white households. Thus, minority households may not have replenished their savings as much as white households or they may have had to draw down their savings even more during the recovery.

Also, financial assets, such as stocks, have recovered in value more quickly than housing since the recession ended. White households are much more likely than minority households to own stocks directly or indirectly through retirement accounts. Thus, they were in better position to benefit from the recovery in financial markets.

All American households since the recovery have started to reduce their ownership of key assets, such as homes, stocks and business equity. But the decrease in asset ownership tended to be proportionally greater among minority households. For example, the homeownership rate for non-Hispanic white households fell from 75.3% in 2010 to 73.9% in 2013, a percentage drop of 2%. Meanwhile, the homeownership rate among minority households decreased from 50.6% in 2010 to 47.4% in 2013, a slippage of 6.5%.

While the current wealth gaps are higher than at the beginning of the recession, they are not at their highest levels as recorded by the Fed's survey. Peak values for the wealth ratios were recorded in the 1989 survey—17 for the white-to-black ratio and 14 for the white-to-Hispanic ratio. But those values of the ratios may be anomalies driven by fluctuations in the wealth of the poorest—those with net worth less than $500. Otherwise, the racial and ethnic wealth gaps in 2013 are at or about their highest levels observed in the 30 years for which we have data.

> *"Blacks are also more likely than whites to say they have been unfairly stopped by police (18% vs. 3%) and that they have been treated unfairly in hiring, pay or a job promotion (21% vs. 4%) in the last year."*

Black and White Americans Differ Widely in Their Views on Race Relations

Renee Stepler

In the following viewpoint, the author cites a 2016 Pew Research Center survey to argue that white and black Americans were split over the state of race relations. Over half say more changes are needed to achieve racial equality. Black adults are more likely than whites to say that black Americans are treated less fairly than whites in the workplace, in the criminal justice system, and when applying for loans or mortgages. Black households continue to fall behind white families in many measures of social and economic well-being. Renee Stepler is a research analyst at Pew Research Center.

As you read, consider the following questions:

1. What is the difference in perception between white and black poll respondents of the progress President Barack Obama made in improving race relations?
2. In what areas do black respondents believe they have been treated less fairly than white respondents?
3. What are some of the differences between white and black family structures that were highlighted by the Pew poll?

A new Pew Research Center survey finds profound differences between black and white Americans in how they view the current state of race relations and racial equality and in the ways they experience day-to-day life.

Here are five key takeaways from the new report on race in America:

1. Whites and blacks are split over the current state of race relations and what progress Obama has made on the issue.

About six-in-ten blacks (61%) say race relations are generally bad, while about equal shares of whites say race relations are good as say they're bad. Overall views on race relations are more positive now than they were a year ago, following the unrest in Baltimore over the death of Freddie Gray, a black man who died while in police custody. Even so, the public's views of race relations are more negative now than they have been for much of the 2000s.

Following the election of Barack Obama as the nation's first black president in 2008, many voters were optimistic that his election would lead to better race relations. Today, about a third of Americans (34%) say Obama has made progress on improving race relations, while about three-in-ten (28%) say he has tried but failed to make progress. A quarter say the president has made race relations worse and 8% say he has not addressed race relations. Blacks are far more likely than whites or Hispanics to say Obama has made progress on race relations (51% vs. 28% and 38%, respectively). Among whites, Republicans are particularly likely to say the president has made race relations worse: 63% of white Republicans say this is the case.

2. About six-in-ten Americans (61%) say more changes are needed to achieve racial equality; 30% say the country has already made enough changes.

There's a big race gap on this question: 88% of blacks and seven-in-ten Hispanics say more changes are needed for blacks to have equal rights with whites compared with 53% of whites. Some 38% of whites say the necessary changes have been made.

About four-in-ten blacks (43%) are doubtful that the country will *ever* make the changes needed for blacks to have equal rights with whites. Just 11% of whites and 17% of Hispanics share this view.

3. By large margins, black adults are more likely than whites to say that blacks are treated less fairly than whites across key areas of American life.

For example, 64% of black adults say blacks are treated less fairly than whites in the workplace, compared with 22% of whites who say the same—a 42-percentage-point gap. Blacks are also considerably more likely than whites—by margins of at least 20 points—to say that blacks are treated less fairly than whites in dealing with the police, in the courts, when applying for a loan or mortgage, in stores and restaurants and when voting in elections.

Blacks are also more likely than whites to say they have experienced unfair treatment because of their race or ethnicity in the past year. Some 47% of blacks say someone has acted as if they were suspicious of them and 45% say people have acted as if they thought they weren't smart. About one-in-ten whites report having these types of experiences. Blacks are also more likely than whites to say they have been unfairly stopped by police (18% vs.

THERE IS NO POST-RACIAL AMERICA

The term post-racial is almost never used in earnest. Instead it's usually employed by talk-show hosts and news anchors looking to measure progress in the Obama era. Earnest or not, the questions we ask matter. As many of our sharper activists and writers have pointed out, America's struggle is to become not post-racial, but post-racist. Put differently, we should seek not a world where the black race and the white race live in harmony, but a world in which the terms black and white have no real political meaning. The Obama-era qualifier is also inherently flawed, because it assumes that the long struggle that commenced when the first enslaved African arrived on American soil centuries ago could somehow be resolved in an instant, by the mere presence of a man who is not a king. These two flaws, taken together, expose a kind of fear, not of having a "conversation about race" but of asking the right questions about racism.

"There is No Post-Racial America," Ta-Nehisi Coates, *Atlantic*, July/August, 2015.

3%) and that they have been treated unfairly in hiring, pay or a job promotion (21% vs. 4%) in the last year.

4. About four-in-ten Americans express support for the Black Lives Matter movement, but blacks are considerably more likely to do so than whites or Hispanics.

About two-thirds of blacks (65%) say they strongly or somewhat support the movement, compared with 40% of whites and 32% of Hispanics.

Among whites, Democrats and those younger than 30 are more likely than others to say they support the Black Lives Matter movement. Fully 64% of white Democrats express support for the movement—roughly equal to the share of black Democrats

(65%). By comparison, 20% of white Republicans and 42% of white independents say they support it.

Similarly, six-in-ten white adults younger than 30 express at least some support for the Black Lives Matter movement, compared with fewer than half of whites who are 30 or older.

Among blacks, there is stronger support for Black Lives Matter from those younger than 50: Roughly half of blacks ages 18 to 29 (52%) and 30 to 49 (47%) *strongly* support the movement, compared with 32% of blacks ages 50 to 64 and 26% of blacks ages 65 and older.

5. Across several measures, black-white gaps in social and economic well-being persist. Blacks lag behind whites in homeownership, household wealth and median income, among other indicators. And these differences remain even when controlling for levels of education

Long-standing racial differences in family structure also persist. Today, non-marital births are more than twice as common among black mothers as white mothers, and black children are nearly three times as likely as white children to be living with a single parent.

> *"Why does race continue to haunt us, 150 years after the Civil War, 50 years after the landmark civil rights legislation of the mid-1960s, and six years into the Obama presidency?"*

White Moderates Have Stopped Fighting for Racial Justice

Christopher Sebastian Parker and Megan Ming Francis

In the following viewpoint, the authors assert that white moderate conservatives have dropped out of the fight for racial equality. Following a series of high-profile killings of black victims, polls find that Americans' perceptions of progress in race relations have deteriorated since the election of Barack Obama as president. One cause may be that white political conservatives have refused to assert themselves as they did during the civil rights period of the 1960s. Some commentators blame members of the Tea Party for their refusal to compromise on policies that might provide more educational and economic opportunities for black Americans. Christopher Sebastian Parker is associate professor of political science at the University of Washington. Megan Ming Francis is assistant professor of political science at the University of Washington.

"Why the Silence of Moderate Conservatives is Dangerous for Race Relations," Christopher Sebastian Parker and Megan Ming Francis, Conversation, August 11, 2015. https://theconversation.com/why-the-silence-of-moderate-conservatives-is-dangerous-for-race-relations-45480. Licensed under CC BY ND 4.0 International.

As you read, consider the following questions:

1. What parallel do the authors see between the Obama administration and the civil rights period of the 1960s?

2. Why do the authors think that white political conservatives are key to resolving racial conflict in the United States?

3. What impact have political groups such as the Tea Party had on the racial climate in the United States?

The past two years of racial turmoil have removed any and all doubt about the continuing significance of race in the United States.

Both whites and blacks have exhibited increasingly negative views on race relations since 2011. A recent New York Times/CBS News poll finds that Americans' perceptions of racial progress have drastically deteriorated over the last year.

The current racial environment stands in stark contrast to 2008, when numerous commentators mused about a post-racial America.

We believe the post-racial narrative began to lose substantial support after George Zimmerman eluded incarceration for the murder of Trayvon Martin, reached a flashpoint with the shooting of unarmed Michael Brown in Ferguson by a police officer, continued to lose steam with the high-profile killings of blacks such as Freddie Gray and Rekia Boyd and was permanently disabled after the grisly massacre of nine black church members in Charleston, South Carolina.

Beyond such headline-grabbing events, race also affects the likelihood of obtaining a job, how one is treated at every stage in the criminal justice system and even health outcomes.

Why does race continue to haunt us, 150 years after the Civil War, 50 years after the landmark civil rights legislation of the mid-1960s, and six years into the Obama presidency?

The persistence of racism, we argue, rests in no small part on the inability of moderate conservatives—from politicians like

Speaker of the House John Boehner to columnists like The New York Times' David Brooks—to recognize the ways in which it continues to affect the life chances of blacks.

We have been here before.

As social scientists well-versed in the history of the civil rights era and the backlash against it, we see a direct parallel between today's conservative moderates and those of the Jim Crow South to whom Martin Luther King Jr addressed his famous Letter from Birmingham Jail in 1963.

The Birmingham Campaign

"If you win in Birmingham, as Birmingham goes, so goes the nation."

These were the words that longtime activist Reverend Fred Shuttlesworth used to encourage King and the Southern Christian Leadership Conference (SCLC) to come to Birmingham and take part in nonviolent direct action protests against segregation.

When they arrived, King, Shuttlesworth and the SCLC launched a formal campaign called Project C (C for confrontation) in which —through sit-ins at lunch counters and marches on City Hall— nonviolent protesters let Birmingham and the rest of the nation know that the city's days of treating blacks as second-class citizens needed to end.

Attempting to quell the momentum, Birmingham issued an injunction barring further protests in the city. Two days later, on Good Friday, April 12 1963, King and a group of Birmingham Campaign supporters were arrested after they openly defied the injunction.

While in jail, King reflected on the slow pace of racial progress and placed the dire situation squarely at the feet of white moderates.

Southern white moderates: a sacred middle ground

Letter from Birmingham Jail was written in response to a Call For Unity, a public statement by eight white clergymen who acknowledged that American racism was wrong but argued that direct action—protest in the streets—was too extreme.

They favored a less confrontational strategy—one that took place in the courts, an approach they hoped would avoid inciting further hatred and violence on the part of white reactionaries.

King's letter does a skillful job in unmasking this type of lukewarm moderate support for civil rights and recasts it as shortsighted, condescending and ultimately dangerous to the black freedom movement.

King is particularly critical of white moderates who disapprove of black anger while turning a blind eye to the circumstances responsible for the anger. He explains:

> You deplore the demonstrations that are presently taking place in Birmingham. But I am sorry that your statement did not express a similar concern for the conditions that brought the demonstrations into being.

Expressing grave disappointment, King ultimately concludes,

> the Negro's great stumbling block in his stride toward freedom is not the White Citizen's Counciler or the Ku Klux Klanner, but the white moderate, who is more devoted to "order" than to justice.

Finally, the letter calls into question the tired refrain of "wait" for change, as moderates often believed blacks were impatient about the pace of progress.

In one of the most cited passages, King writes, "This 'Wait' has almost always meant 'Never.'"

Moderates occupied a sacred middle ground between the progressives and the reactionaries in the South, and King wanted their support.

He would not get it.

Southern reactionaries, led by Eugene (Bull) Connor, commissioner of public safety in Birmingham, feeling the ground shake beneath them, did not flinch in their defense of white supremacy.

Aided by the silence of southern moderates, the reactionary white establishment felt it had a green light to inflict harm on the black community.

With the world watching, they turned high-pressure fire hoses on black students, allowed police dogs to attack demonstrators and arrested over 1,000 nonviolent protesters.

The violent events in Birmingham were instrumental in showing an international and a domestic audience the ugly side of American racism.

Soon after, moderate whites beyond the South became a key force in drumming up support for the Civil Rights Act of 1964.

2015: moderate conservatives are still key

Fast forwarding to today, the racial climate is eerily similar to what we observed more than 50 years ago.

However, now it's the entire country, not just the South, that is riven with racial violence.

This time around, as one of us together with Matt A Barreto show in our book Change They Can't Believe In, it's the Tea Party pushing a reactionary agenda. And, much like their forebears during Jim Crow, moderate conservatives, who are relatively progressive on race, refuse to assert themselves where race is concerned.

If David Brooks, who has castigated the Tea Party for their refusal to compromise and for having "no sense of moral decency," represents the sentiments of moderate conservatives, it's easy to see why race remains a problem in America.

Consider the following.

We analyzed data from the American National Election Study (2012) to investigate the distribution of reactionary relative to establishment conservatives among self-identified conservatives in the American electorate.

Our analysis indicates that approximately 22% of all conservatives identify strongly with the Tea Party. This means that approximately 78% of all conservatives are at least moderate.

But what do they say on race?

In his recent review of Ta-Nehisi Coates' latest book, Between the World and Me, in The New York Times, Brooks essentially rejects the notion that the racial animus that results in violence remains a problem when he writes,

> I think you [Coates] distort American history. This country, like each person in it, is a mixture of glory and shame. There's…a Harlem Children's Zone for every KKK—and usually vastly more than one.

The effects of racism, in other words, at least these days, are mitigated by the opportunities this great country provides everyone. One way to read Brooks is that he is saying that race and racism are not as bad as Coates, and by extension, black folk, believe it is.

Similarly, John Boehner, speaker of the house and part of the conservative leadership, has downplayed racism—most recently in his response to Donald Trump's inflammatory comments about Mexicans.

And while far too many moderate conservatives sit by, it is the reactionaries who commandeer the racial agenda with, for instance, their lionizing of George Zimmerman and their dismissal of protesters in Ferguson as "blacks out of control" and "aboriginals."

We believe this nation is, as it was in the 1960s during the Birmingham Campaign, at a crossroads in race relations.

The reality on the ground is that blacks are dying at an alarming rate at the hands of agents of the state (law enforcement) as well as individual white citizens like George Zimmerman and Dylann Roof.

Combating such injustice will require moderate conservatives to take a bold stand.

We agree with King: moderates must not shrink in the presence of vocal white reactionaries or hide behind lofty color-blind rhetoric.

As King affirmed over 50 years ago,

> Injustice anywhere is a threat to justice everywhere.

> *"Cities continue to exhibit high levels of neighborhood inequality and poverty."*

With Urban Gentrification Racial Inequality Remains

Jackelyn Hwang

In the following viewpoint, the author argues that gentrification has not improved diversity in the nation's large cities. Recent research shows that white populations moving into cities from the suburbs are choosing white neighborhoods in which to live, bypassing black areas. Economically blighted neighborhoods have remained disadvantaged. Jackelyn Hwang is Assistant Professor of Sociology at Stanford University, specializing in the persistence of neighborhood inequality by race.

As you read, consider the following questions:

1. What is gentrification?
2. What city's neighborhoods did the author study?
3. Which immigrant presence was perceived as more positive?

"How 'Gentrification' in American Cities Maintains Racial Inequality and Segregation," Jackelyn Hwang, Journalist's Resource, August 20, 2014. http://journalistsresource.org/ studies/society/race-society/gentrification-american-cities-racial-inequality-segregation-research-brief. Licensed under CC BY 3.0.

After decades of population declines, cities are adding population more rapidly than suburbs for the first time in nearly a century, as trendy middle-class neighborhoods continue to grow in number and size across areas that more affluent Americans once considered places to avoid. Yet research tells us that American cities continue to exhibit high levels of neighborhood inequality and poverty, especially for racial minorities. My research seeks to understand these two seemingly contradictory trends by examining how gentrification unfolds over time. Do neighborhoods gentrify at the same pace or to the same degree? Does gentrification spread evenly into its adjacent disinvested neighborhoods? If not, what factors influence these differences—leaving some urban areas mired in extreme poverty?

My research with sociologist, SSN scholar and Harvard colleague Robert Sampson examined these issues in a study of Chicago neighborhoods. We define gentrification as the reinvestment and renewal of previously debilitated urban neighborhoods that occurs as middle- and upper-middle-class residents move in. To measure neighborhood change, we went beyond traditional sources of Census data to use information on the location of institutions and urban amenities, police data, community surveys, and—most innovative of all—visual information from Google Street View. The visible streetscape of neighborhoods provides direct indicators of change, such as new construction, rehabilitation, and beautification efforts. By assessing the presence of our various indicators of gentrification for nearly 2,000 blocks, we were able to measure degrees of gentrification for neighborhoods of varying racial composition. Additional research I have done also probes the impact of immigration.

Minority neighborhoods are not readily gentrified

Neighborhood selection is an important reason that poor enclaves and racial segregation persist in U.S. cities. Racial and ethnic stereotypes influence people's choices about where they want to live and which neighborhoods to avoid—and people

AMERICANS THINK RACIAL DIVIDE IS GROWING

Most Americans think that race relations in the U.S. are bad, and a substantial minority believe they are getting worse, according to the results of a New York Times/CBS News poll published Thursday.

The poll, which surveyed 1,205 people from across the country, asked respondents about a number of racial concerns. It found that about six in 10 Americans—57 percent—viewed race relations as being "generally bad," a figure slightly down from the last month the poll was conducted in April, but at least 13 points higher than poll findings in earlier months.

Both blacks and whites view race relations negatively—with 40 percent of both groups saying relations were getting worse, almost double the amount of all respondents who said that they were improving. The level of discontent about race relations among blacks has now soared to 68 percent, the highest level during the Obama presidency, and close to the numbers recorded in the aftermath of the riots that followed the acquittal of Los Angeles police officers charged in the beating of Rodney King in 1992.

"Race Relations in US: Many Americans Think Racial Divide Growing, Relations Getting Worse: Poll," Mark Hanrahan, *International Business Times*, July 24, 2015.

also consider crime, property values, school quality, and local amenities. In popular media and political debates, gentrification is often depicted as a process in which middle-class whites move into and thus integrate minority neighborhoods. But in fact, gentrifiers prefer already white neighborhoods; they are least attracted to black neighborhoods and see Asian and Latino neighborhoods as middling options.

We analyzed shifts over time in or near debilitated Chicago neighborhoods that had showed signs of gentrification in 1995. Race and neighborhood reputations turned out to play an important role, as gentrification proceeded more slowly through

2009 in areas with higher shares of blacks and Latinos. Even after we took into account other important factors such as crime, poverty, and proximity to amenities, neighborhoods with more blacks and Latinos were less likely to continue to gentrify or even to reverse course and decline after early signs of transformation. Gentrification also tends to slow down in the face of perceptions of disorder in a neighborhood, even if the actual level of disorder does not match perceptions.

Sometimes gentrification does affect areas with racial and ethnic diversity, but we saw little such change in Chicago neighborhoods where more than 40 percent of residents were black. Only neighborhoods that were at least 35 percent white continued to gentrify after 1995.

The impact of Asian and Latino immigration

Immigration has increased sharply in recent decades, shifting the ethnic and racial composition of many urban neighborhoods—sometimes boosting housing demand and creating new local businesses. To look at immigration and gentrification, I tracked demographic and socioeconomic changes since the 1970s in economically struggling neighborhoods identified in 23 large U.S. cities. Tellingly, the neighborhoods that gentrified were overwhelmingly multiethnic in the 1970s, and remained relatively diverse over the next few decades. But the ethnic specifics mattered. An early presence of Asians and rising proportions of Asian residents tended to be positively associated with gentrification, while the same was not true for a growing Hispanic presence. Contrasts were stronger when blacks were a major presence. What is more, in cities where Hispanics had a well-established presence, economically distressed neighborhoods continued to struggle as more Hispanics moved in.

Consider Seattle compared to Chicago. Seattle had a much less diverse population and has only recently become an immigrant destination, while Chicago has served as a major gateway for many decades, particularly for Latinos who make up nearly one-third of its population. Data for Chicago neighborhoods reveal that Latino neighborhoods have experienced little or slowed rates of gentrification. But in Seattle, influxes of immigrants, often Asians, have furthered neighborhood gentrification.

Implications for racial inequality and urban policy

In sum, gentrification in U.S. cities has been problematic for low-income minorities, and not just because new middle-class residents displace poor people. Despite gentrification in some locales, economically blighted black neighborhoods, plus those with growing Hispanic populations, have tended to remain disadvantaged. Some neighborhoods that attracted Asian immigrants experienced ethnic diversification along with gentrification, but the arrival of more Latinos has gone hand in hand with gentrification only in cities where Latinos are not already negatively stigmatized.

In many of America's cities, civic leaders have pinned hopes for urban revitalization on gentrification and efforts to attract immigrants. But facts on the ground show that they need to weigh the probability that these forms of urban change can further isolate poor blacks and Latinos and—contrary to media claims—actually increase racial segregation and inequality. Urban policymakers should take note: Fresh thinking is needed to devise targeted, sustained efforts to protect minorities from displacement, ensure affordable housing for those with low incomes, and further the economic revitalization of blighted urban neighborhoods. Gentrification and immigration are not panaceas.

Periodical and Internet Sources Bibliography

The following articles have been selected to supplement the diverse views presented in this chapter.

Jennifer Agiesta and Sonya Ross, "AP poll: Majority harbor prejudice against blacks," Associated Press, October 27, 2012.

Michael A. Fletcher, "Fifty years after March on Washington, economic gap between blacks, whites persists," *Washington Post*, August 28, 2013.

Nikole Hannah-Jones, "Segregation Now: The Resegregation of America's Schools," *ProPublica*, April 16, 2014.

P. Katel, "Race relations," *CQ researcher*, May 20, 2015

Randall Kennedy, "The civil rights movement and the politics of memory: as opportunities try to hijack the Movement's legacy, let's remember what actually occurred," *American Prospect*, Spring 2015.

Tami Lubby, "Worsening wealth inequality by race," *CNN Money*, June 21, 2012.

Barack Obama, "Remarks by the President at the 50th Anniversary of the Selma to Montgomery Marches," White House, March 7, 2015.

Joshua Rothman, "The Origins of 'Privilege,'" *New Yorker*, May 12, 2014.

Lydia Saad, "U.S. Mood on Economy Up, Race Relations Sharply Down," Gallup, January 19, 2015.

Ilyasah Shabazz, "What Would Malcolm X Think?" *New York Times*, February 20, 2015.

George Yancy, "Dear White America," *New York Times*, December 24, 2015.

OPPOSING
VIEWPOINTS®
SERIES

CHAPTER 2

Is Race Overemphasized?

Chapter Preface

Sociologists in the United States use a variety of colorful metaphors to describe the cultural diversity of the country: melting pot, stew, salad bowl, kaleidoscope, mosaic. These terms refer to the people of different ethnicities who have made the United States their home. Though social scientists acknowledge the range of skin colors reflecting the geographic origins of various populations, a word they dislike using is "race." Race is a social construct, they explain. Skin color is an adaptation to living either near to or far from the equator and the intense radiation from the sun. Skin color says nothing else about a person other than a geographical heritage.

While experts may view race as an illusion and skin color as a biological variation, some Americans see race as a very real method to stratify society. Race is used to create a hierarchy, a system of haves and have nots, based on the lightness or darkness of one's skin. Those who study geography and urban environments can see the stratification of society in the rings of affluent white suburbs surrounding poorer minority families left in decaying inner cities.

However, urban planners have been documenting a phenomenon called gentrification in these aging urban cores. Hip young professionals, looking for housing bargains and a short commute to their downtown offices, started fixing up dilapidated neighborhoods and moving in. Housing tightened and rents increased, pricing out the original residents and leaving them nowhere to go.

The stresses of poverty, unemployment, drugs, and gangs have created environments that often lead to crime. Cities have taken varying approaches to policing the violence produced by crime. Some of these approaches have been effective; some have opened police forces up to accusations of racism. The Black Lives Matter movement grew out of high profile and often fatal confrontations between police and black teens and men.

The intense media coverage of these confrontations has caused many people to scrutinize the media itself. Some media critics accuse media outlets such as television networks and Internet web sites of disproportionately covering minority violence at the expense of crime perpetuated by white people. This coverage creates and reinforces negative stereotypes that can prevent progress and opportunity for minority children and teens. Debate also rages about the negative images of Native Americans that are spread by the sports and film industries. This debate is leading some sports teams to find new mascots. Hollywood is beginning to take a look at how movies and television portray Indians.

The viewpoints in this chapter show the ways that race is characterized in the United States. Readers will be asked to think about how race is intricately involved in the neighborhoods in which they live, the media they consume, and the privileges they enjoy or lack.

> "*While anthropologists employed discrete categories such as 'black,' 'brown' and 'white,' in actuality, pigmentation grades continuously along a geographic line from the equator to northern and southern latitudes, regardless of race.*"

Race is a Social, Not Scientific Construct

Darren Curnoe

In the following viewpoint, the author states that, although the idea of race seems to be taken for granted by many people today, research into genetics proves that racial categories are arbitrary and subjective. A person's skin color may possibly be a link to a geographical location of origin, but it doesn't represent a genetic category. Genetics does show that most populations reflect a mixed ancestry from a variety of locations. Darren Curnoe is a human evolution specialist and director of the Palaeontology, Geobiology and Earth Archives Research Centre (PANGEA), University of New South Wales, Australia.

"Human Races: Biological Reality or Cultural Delusion," Darren Curnoe, Conversation, August 14, 2014. https://theconversation.com/human-races-biological-reality-or-cultural-delusion-30419. Licensed under CC BY ND 4.0 International.

As you read, consider the following questions:

1. According to the author, how does the concept of race differ from the concept of species?
2. What are some of the features that anthropologists use to determine racial categories?
3. According to the author, what has research into genetics shown us about genetic variation among humans?

The issue of race has been in the news a lot lately with the canning of proposed amendments to Australia's Racial Discrimination Act, attempts by extremists to commit genocide on cultural minorities in Iraq and a new book by US author Nicholas Wade that has scientists claiming their work was hijacked to promote an ideological agenda.

The idea that races are part of our existence and daily experience, especially those of us living in multicultural societies, seems to be just taken for granted by many people.

But are races real or simply social/political constructs? Is there any scientific evidence they exist in humans? Or are some scientists just being politically correct in denying their existence?

Race in nature

Biologists have used the "race" category for hundreds of years to classify varieties of plants and animals and, of course, humans. It has normally been reserved for geographic populations belonging to a single species, and has often been used as a synonym of "subspecies".

While the species concept, or definition, has also had its share of controversies, biologists agree that species are real, not arbitrary. They represent reproductively cohesive evolutionary units.

Yet the use of "race" in biology is far from straightforward. It has been controversial for many decades irrespective of which species it has been applied to; human or otherwise.

Ernst Mayr, one of the intellectual giants of biology during the 20th century and a pioneer of the classification of biological diversity, was critical of the use of races and subspecies by taxonomists.

Unlike species, races and subspecies are very fuzzy categories. They lack a clear definition as a biological rank, being arbitrarily and subjectively defined and applied.

Races have been identified on ecological, geographical, climatic, physiological and even seasonal criteria. There are subraces, local races, race populations and microgeographic and macrogeographic races; even "ethnic taxa".

Races simply aren't real like species are: species represent genuine "breaks" in nature while races are part of a continuum and can only ever have very arbitrary boundaries.

Their lack of favour in biology today has a great deal to do with a desire to remove subjectivity and fuzzy thinking from the enterprise of classifying nature.

A race to the bottom

Scientific racialism has a very chequered history. Many large-scale atrocities and instances of genocide were carried out in the name of race, usually involving notions of the superiority of one race over another, particularly during the 17th through to 20th centuries.

Anthropology was obsessed with race from the 18th to 20th centuries and has a lot to answer for in terms of the part it played in justifying political and ideological racism.

If you doubt for a moment the impact that race has had on many people, just ask an indigenous person anywhere in the world what they think of race.

History doesn't lie

Putting aside the ethics for a moment, is it legitimate from the biological perspective to apply race to humans? We might consider this from two viewpoints:

How would we go about recognising races?

How many races might we then identify?

Both questions were the source of regular consternation during the 20th century, and earlier, as anthropology struggled to make sense of—and pigeonhole—the geographic variation seen in humankind around the world.

What evidence was used to identify human races? Well, as it happens, just about anything, and most of it unscientific.

The book *Races of Africa*, published in three editions from 1930 to 1957, recognised six races inhabiting the African continent. Its author, British anthropologist C G Seligman, readily admitted that the races it described were defined on non-biological grounds, a fact "readers should appreciate in order to make necessary allowances and corrections."

How were these races identified? Mostly using the languages people spoke: as Seligman further informed his readers, "linguistic criteria will play a considerable part in the somewhat mixed classification adopted."

Seligman should be praised for his honesty. Many other anthropologists continued the ruse of biological objectivity well into the 1970s; some stick to it today. The reality is that most races were identified on cultural or linguistic grounds, or simply on account of educated intuition, not biology.

Another fascinating example of the arbitrariness of this category is the so-called "Negrito" "pygmy" race, which sometimes still gets talked about by anthropologists and archaeologists with respect to the origins of indigenous people in East Asia and Australasia.

It has been defined to include people from the Congo of Africa, the Andaman Islands, several Southeast Asian countries, New Guinea and Australia. The Negrito race is not a biological reality reflecting history, but an artificial construct based on superficial similarities.

The skull measurements, brain size estimates, hair form, skin and eye colour, intelligence and blood group data used to justify races were simply retrofitted to each of them.

Moreover, these physical features were very far from flawless in reinforcing established notions of race. None of them has provided any evidence for discrete boundaries between human groups—or groups as genuine geographic entities—and many of them simply reflect the environment, not biological history.

Take skin colour, or pigmentation, as an example, a feature that has been used in almost every racial classification published. While anthropologists employed discrete categories such as "black," "brown" and "white," in actuality, pigmentation grades continuously along a geographic cline from the equator to northern and southern latitudes, regardless of race.

How many races have been recognised for living people? Well, there seems to have been no real limit in practice, reinforcing their arbitrary nature.

During the 20th century, estimates of the number of races varied from two to 200 across the globe. For Europe alone, one book published in 1950 estimated six, while another one the same year identified at least 30 races.

Sure, you might recognise races if you compare the skin pigmentation of people from a village in the Scottish Highlands to one in coastal Kenya. But you'd be kidding yourself because you would be ignoring all of the people who live along the thousands of kilometres that stretch between them who don't fit into your concocted moulds.

Genetics: the final arbitrator

Developments in the field of genetics from the 1960s onwards made new inroads into the question of race. In fact, genetics marked the death knell of the scientific race debate.

Geneticists have found a number of features about human diversity that just don't fit the pattern expected for the ancient subdivisions we might anticipate if races actually existed.

Some important findings that show racial categories to be unfounded include:

- humans are genetically much less diverse than most mammals, including our chimpanzee cousins

- common estimates are that around 2%-8% of genetic variation occurs between large groups living on different continents; a pattern that again contrasts with most mammals, which show much greater differences on continental scales
- living Africans possess substantially more genetic variation than other populations. This reflects the ancestry of our species in Africa—only a couple of hundred thousand years ago—and the establishment of all non-African populations by a small founder group from Africa—less than 60,000 years ago
- most populations show high levels of mixed ancestry indicating that people have migrated regularly in the past, with most groups far from being isolated from each other for any great length of time.

Are we all the same then?

There is no denying that humans are variable. Some of that variation —a small amount—reflects our geographic origins. Genetic data show this unequivocally.

But this is simply not the same as claiming that this geographic variation has been partitioned by nature into discrete units we call races. Humans have simply refused to be classified along taxonomic grounds—beyond the fact that we all belong to the single species *Homo sapiens.*

The facts are that the races recognised by anthropologists during the 19th and 20th centuries simply don't hold up to scrutiny from physical or genetic evidence; besides, races never were scientific to begin with.

> "*Most of us get information from the mainstream media—which blatantly feeds us a biased distortion of the truth, with the wrong information, favoritism toward white people (whether they're murderers or not), and the demonization of people of color (whether they're victims or not).*"

The Media is Biased Against People of Color

Maisha Z. Johnson

In the following viewpoint, Maisha Z. Johnson addresses the role of the media in perceptions about race. Most Americans get their information from the mainstream media, which some people think is biased against people of color. White people who are responsible for violence against black people are described in very different ways than are racial minorities who commit crimes. This distortion perpetuates racism and upholds white privilege. Maisha Z. Johnson is a writer and activist.

"8 Ways the Media Upholds White Privilege and Demonizes People of Color," Maisha Z. Johnson, Everyday Feminism, July 22, 2015. Reprinted by permission.

As you read, consider the following questions:

1. According to the author, how do the media stereotype people of color compared to how white people are characterized?
2. According to the author, how do the media discredit activist and justice movements by people of color, compared to the activism of white people?
3. What are some of the strategies media consumers can use to counteract media bias against people of color?

A re you paying attention to how the media gives you information? Sandra Bland, a 28-year-old Black woman who had spoken out against police violence, died in police custody on July 13 after a routine traffic stop.

Local authorities ruled her death a suicide.

The people who knew Bland are skeptical of that version of events, and a newly released video showing a Texas state trooper aggressively arresting her has cast widespread doubt. We don't know the details, but some of the relevant information was already filled in before Bland's death.

Like the fact that the county where Bland died has a vicious history of racism that includes the district attorney's office and the standing sheriff, who was fired from his previous post for racism.

Like the statistics that show how police target people of color for stops, arrests, and incarceration, and are far more likely to use force against them.

Like the fact that Bland was a Black woman living in a country, state, and county where racist violence has been weaved into everyday life since the day Bland was born, and for *centuries* before that.

But one media outlet chose to frame the narrative this way: "Woman Found Dead in Jail Cell Had Prior Run-Ins With Law."

It's true—Sandra Bland had been pulled over like this before. Several of those "run-ins" were citations for *unpaid traffic tickets*.

Her last encounter with police was the fatal one, but like other people of color who are targets, it wasn't the only one.

If you weren't paying attention, you might think a dangerous hardened criminal—not the real Sandra Bland—had just died in jail.

Were you paying attention when the media told you about last month's racist mass murder in Charleston, South Carolina?

On June 17th, a white man seeking to kill Black people walked into Emanuel AME Church, sat through Bible Study with the congregants, and then massacred all of them but one. He stole nine innocent lives.

While the mainstream media that so many of us consume covered that much, it didn't have a complete analysis of why this happened—and that's not enough.

Dylann Roof acted on his belief in white supremacy. And on inspiration from George Zimmerman, the man who was acquitted for killing unarmed Black teenager Travyon Martin. And further on complicit support from friends who did nothing when they heard him tell racist jokes and talk about starting a "race war."

He acted on the anti-Black hatred and fear generated from stereotypes of Black people as sexual predators. On strategies of white supremacist groups active in the US today—strategies that have continued with arson attacks on multiple Black churches since the massacre.

He acted on biases that the media perpetuates every day.

This was a mass murder supported by a white supremacist system that intersects with our daily lives. Unfortunately, he's not the last to violently lash out with this support.

So after incidents like the attacks against the Charleston congregants and Sandra Bland, we need to pay attention to how the media participates in this dangerous system, and demand some crucial changes.

To have any hope of preventing and healing from this type of horrendous violence, we have to deliberately and ferociously take on the racism that prevails in our country to allow this to happen.

But the way we get our information about tragedies like this one skews our beliefs about what happened, why, and what we should do about it.

Most of us get information from the mainstream media—which blatantly feeds us a biased distortion of the truth, with the wrong information, favoritism toward white people (whether they're murderers or not), and the demonization of people of color (whether they're victims or not).

If you think of the news as simply reporting what you need to know, then you're missing the fact that it's reinforcing a basic idea of white supremacy: that white people are more valuable than people of color.

It's just like other instances of racism—sometimes it's obvious and you can easily point out that it's wrong. But a lot of the time, it's subtle, playing right into the implicit biases you don't even know you have to make you believe in ideas you don't even realize are racist.

It's a disgusting manipulation of the public that lets everyday racism go unchecked.

So instead of buying into the media's biases as people of color lose their lives to racist violence, let's pay attention to the following examples of how the media upholds white privilege.

1. They Show White People's Accomplishments —And People of Color's Alleged Crimes

We rely on the media to provide the details of who suspects and victims are.

Regardless of what defines someone's story if they make it on the news—whether they've committed a heinous act or fallen victim to violence—we're all dynamic human beings made up of more than a single incident. We've all had accomplishments and made mistakes.

So the media chooses which parts of our lives to show—and their choices often humanize white people while villifying people of color.

For instance, young white men responsible for horrible mass shootings are often given the "brilliant loner" treatment. Headlines describing killers like Adam Lanza and James Holmes as "smart," "quiet," and "nice" are common.

On the other hand, when young people of color are the victims of violence, they still rarely get their accomplishments named in the mainstream media.

In McKinney, Texas, white neighbors yelled racial slurs and physically assaulted a group of youth of color at a pool party—and things got even worse when a police officer called to the scene wrestled unarmed Black teenager Dejerria Becton to the ground, pulled a gun on her friends, and sat on her to restrain her.

So when Fox News's Megyn Kelly talked about that horrible incident, she could've researched Dejerria Becton's achievements. She could've focused on the fact that Dejerria was an innocent party who was invited to the honorable act of celebrating a friend's graduation, AND who was following the officer's instructions before he attacked her.

Instead, Kelly said that the girl was "no saint," so rather than seeing her as an innocent victim of violence, viewers can believe that this young girl had it coming.

2. They Choose Charming Photos of White Victims—And "Incriminating" Photos of Victims of Color

In addition to words, the media's images have a huge influence on how we view people.

And once again, the media makes a choice—because we've all taken pictures that make us look impressive, and we've taken ones that people could use to make us look like we were up to no good.

When Twitter users started trending the hashtag #IfTheyGunnedMeDown, they highlighted how much the media makes different choices depending on race.

When white victims lose their lives, the media shows graduation pictures, family photos, positive images of the life lost.

They even often use such images for white suspects and murderers, giving us a sense of who they were before things went terribly wrong. Theater shooter James Holmes was shown in a smiling senior photo wearing a suit and tie below a headline calling him "a brilliant science student."

When mainstream media outlets broke the story of Michael Brown's slaying at the hands of the police, they could have used photographs from his recent high school graduation. Instead, many of them chose an image that showed him towering over the camera, holding his hand in what some people on social media interpreted as a gang sign.

Clearly, this media representation sways the conversation about whether or not the police were justified in killing the unarmed teenager. A one-dimensional representation of a victim as a criminal makes us more likely to believe that the killers' actions were necessary.

3. They Empathize With the "Motivation" for a White Person's Violence

Ever heard someone say "Wait until we get all the facts" before deciding how to judge a violence incident?

When we get these "facts" from the mainstream media, they encourage us to hold off judgment until we know what's "really" going on.

And sometimes, even in cases of blatant racially biased violence, their narrative about what's going on is based on empathy for the white perpetrator's "motivations."

For example, in the case of Dylann Roof, who killed those nine church-goers in Charleston for no reason other than that they are Black, some reporters said "we don't know why he did it." Others called it "an attack on religious freedom."

Clearly, their hesitation to state the obvious influenced some people, who accused leaders speaking out about the racism— rather than the mass murderer who wanted to "start a race war"—of being the ones "making everything about race." If the media is so concerned about people's motivations, you'd think they would've focused on what drove a Black man named Jim Jones to sacrifice his life by shielding his mother from bullets.

Instead, they called Jones a "son with a troubled past," as Twitter user Rashad Alaiyan pointed out when he placed that headline side-by-side with one that described Dylann Roof as a "loner" who was "caught in 'Internet evil.'"

This empathy for white attackers has the dangerous effect of encouraging us to look away from what's really going on, and focus instead on the well-being of the person who committed a horrible act.

4. They Emphasize That a "Hateful" White Person Acted Alone—While Casting People of Color as Stereotypes of Their Race

I'm not saying the media always shows empathy for white offenders.

There have been times when the mainstream media rightfully characterizes a white murderer as a person who did something terrible, showing empathy for the victims, regardless of their killer's motivations.

But it's also telling that in these cases, white offenders are often characterized as a "lone wolf," someone who acted alone on their own hate.

Media outlets included descriptions of white supremacist Larry Steve McQuilliams, who thankfully killed no one in his Texas shooting rampage, as a lone wolf.

According to the Southern Poverty Law Center, 74% of domestic terrorist acts planned or carried out were the work of people working alone, with just one or two people behind 90% of them.

Violent racist extremists like McQuilliams fall into those categories, but the mainstream media rarely calls them "terrorists." That word is usually reserved for mass murderers identified as Muslim extremists—especially those who are Arab.

This, in spite of the fact that people like white supremacists have killed almost twice as many people in the US as Muslim extremists who represent "terrorism" to so many Americans.

The media's framing of terrorism often spreads Islamophobic ideas, perpetuating stereotypes that put the safety of Arab Americans —and anyone who's seen to fit the erroneous stereotypes —at risk.

As we've seen since 9/11, when the media conflates Islam with terrorism, incidents of Islamophobic violence against innocent people rise.

Unlike with white suspects indoctrinated by violent white supremacist ideology, the mainstream media doesn't mull over "why he did it" if a suspect is an Arab man. And they don't even write him off as an evil lone wolf.

The media upholds the white privilege of not having the most violent people of your race appear as a stereotype of you.

And what a difference that makes—if white people who commit racist violence are just lone wolves, that means we don't have to recognize the fact that they're following a legacy embedded in our country's violent history.

We don't have to face the whole system of white supremacy, or be accountable for the fact that it's not just the violent lone wolves who participate—it's also everyday people with good intentions, like you and me.

5. They Humanize the "Troubled" Lives of White Suspects

In addition to considering motivation, the media also humanizes white suspects by focusing on their struggles.

Details mentioned far more often for white suspects than suspects of color include if they were "bullied," or "kept to themselves," or "had a hard home life."

Santa Barbara shooter Elliot Rodger is one of many mass murderers whose mental health was the also focus of a lot of media coverage. Rodger, who is half white and half Malaysian Chinese, benefits from white privilege and this is an example of how.

Calling white male suspects "mentally ill" instead of examining other factors is a pattern in the media, and it does twice the injustice: shifting the blame away from the person who chose to commit violent acts, and reinforcing stigma about people with mental illness.

Having a mental illness doesn't mean someone's predisposed to violence. So framing the story this way is a harmful distraction and a benefit given only to white suspects.

When the suspect is a person of color, the media often uncovers criminal records, not medical records.

And once again, even victims of color don't get the humanizing efforts to detail the causes of the troubling aspects of their backgrounds.

With so many poor people of color losing their lives to police violence, for instance, then why doesn't the mainstream media talk about their struggles that lead to fatal encounters with police?

For example, Freddie Gray, who died in Baltimore police custody, grew up as one of thousands of low-income African-Americans exposed to deadly chemicals in an inner city home.

His family won a settlement after arguing that the lead poisoning he and his sister got "played a significant part in their educational, behavioral, and medical problems."

Add up the traumatic effect of poverty and mass incarceration in poor Black neighborhoods with the experience of growing up as a Black male targeted by police, and you can understand why we need to address the deadly risk of criminalizing poor people of color. But that's not what the mainstream media talks about.

6. They Use Innocence and Youth to Humanize White Suspects—And Treat Young Victims of Color as Older and Guilty

When suspects are young, the difference in how the mainstream media treats them is clear.

News Coverage of African-American Crime May Be Lopsided

In stories where race could be identified, the percentage of African-American suspects in murders, thefts, and assaults covered by WCBS, WNBC, WABC, and WNYW was well above the percentage of African-American suspects who have been arrested for those crimes in New York City. According to averages of arrest statistics from the New York City Police Department (NYPD) for the past four years, African-American suspects were arrested in 54 percent of murders, 55 percent of thefts, and 49 percent of assaults. Meanwhile, over the past three months, the suspects in the four stations' coverage of murders were 68 percent African-American, the suspects in their coverage of thefts were 80 percent African-American, and the suspects in their coverage of assaults were 72 percent African-American.

"REPORT: New York City Television Stations Give Lopsided Coverage to Black Crime," Todd Gregory, Salvatore Colleluori, and Daniel Angster, Media Matters, August 26, 2014.

Studies show implicit biases lead many of us to see innocent Black children as guilty adults.

And it's no wonder that our impression depends on the child's race, when the source of much of our information—the mainstream media—reminds us that young white suspects are "kids."

Even Adam Lanza, the 20-year-old who killed children in Newton, Connecticut, was described in headlines as a "deeply disturbed kid."

Tamir Rice, on the other hand, is a 12 year old Black boy who was playing with a toy gun when he was killed by police less than two seconds after their arrival.

Tamir was the victim in this case, the one who tragically lost his life. But when the media calls him a "young man" and reminds us that he was "big for his age," they're not just reporting information on the tragic death of a child.

They're not talking about why police are twenty-one times more likely to kill young Black men than young white men.

In fact, they're helping justify violence and mass incarceration against youth of color, by characterizing them as dangerous criminals, whether they're victims or not.

7. They Discredit Justice Movements for People of Color—And Give Rioting White People a Pass

Not everyone's buying the media's biased stories.

Racial justice activists put blood, sweat, and tears into advocating for justice for victims of color, and their voices help bring attention to the truth about racism.

Unfortunately, many of us have to filter through bias to hear activist voices, too.

And there's a huge difference between how the media portrays mass gatherings advocating for people of color and those with groups of white people.

Protests for Freddie Gray in Baltimore, for instance, were part of a national grassroots movement, Black Lives Matter. They included dynamic speakers, wise youth leaders, deep analyses of issues of inequality, and even a Michael Jackson impersonator dancing to "show positivity" and raise money for the Gray family.

Pretty impressive, right?

But that wasn't the impression you would've gotten from watching or reading coverage of the protests in the mainstream media.

Their coverage was focused almost entirely on "riots," "looting," and "destruction." After 10,000 marched peacefully one day, the next morning's headlines included words like "chaos," "destruction," and "violence" to talk about the few agitators who strayed from the protest to vandalize.

The media blew the vandalism out of proportion, spread inaccurate information about how the chaotic moments began, and used one word over and over again to characterize the protesters, the vast majority of whom were advocating for peace.

That word was "thugs."

Clearly, not just anyone who gathers in mass or causes destruction gets called a "thug" in the media. If that were the case, then white people who destroy things in the name of sports or who riot over pumpkins would get the same treatment, but the media doesn't portray those people as dangerous criminals.

Even when mobs of white people are committing violent crimes, the media doesn't treat them this way.

White biker gangs in Waco, Texas beat, stabbed, and shot each other, and fired at police, in a bloody brawl that resulted in nine deaths. The media called it a "rumble," and a "meeting" to "settle their differences"—and the word "thug" was noticeably absent.

This double standard isn't just unfair—it's also holding back progress in the fight against racial injustice.

A recent study found that white Americans believe protesting improves the nation—unless Black folks are the ones protesting. That's the dangerous impact of the media's bias.

The more people believe the mainstream media's idea that activists of color are "destroying their own neighborhoods" with unwarranted protests, the harder we have to fight to spread the word about the change we need.

8. They Put Victims of Color at Fault—And White Suspects in Self-Defense Mode

If it seems like white attackers had no choice but to defend themselves with violence, that also helps to justify violence against people of color in the public's eyes.

The media sets the stage for this narrative with biases that lead us to see people of color as guilty, and they can really drive it home with as little as a hint that a victim of color was at fault for their own attack.

For example, African-American teenager Renisha McBride was reportedly asking for help after a car accident in a mostly-white neighborhood, and Theodore Wafer had no reason to kill her. But he did, and the media focused on whether or not she was drunk at the time of her murder "—in spite of the fact that she likely posed no threat to the shooter.

South Carolina Officer Michael Slager also had no reason to kill Walter Scott. And at first, the news reported his version of the events that led him to shoot Scott in "self-defense."

It wasn't until after a civilian's video of the shooting was released that the media reported on the real story: Slager shot Walter Scott in the back as he ran away, posing absolutely no threat to the officer. He then put his taser beside Scott's body to make it look like self-defense, and lied about it.

And the media ate it up and fed it to us.

What else are we missing when we believe the mainstream media's stories without thinking critically about their biases?

The bad news is that this all shows just how deeply white privilege and racism are ingrained in the everyday media we consume.

The good news is that many of these examples also show that we have the power to resist the media's biased messages and get to the truth.

In this digital age, people are recording incidents of police brutality and harassment, forcing us to confront what's really going on when an unarmed victim is no longer alive to tell their side of the story.

We're participating on social media with hashtags like #AliveWhileBlack and #CrimingWhileWhite, to show how the mainstream media's narrative doesn't reflect what it means to be targeted because you're Black, or granted the benefit of the doubt because you're white.

We're speaking up and spreading the word when the mainstream media demonizes people of color, and telling our own stories about who we are.

You can help, by amplifying the voices of people speaking out.

For the love of justice, turn off the mainstream news channels and support alternative media instead. Seek out the information that's on the ground with grassroots organizations analyzing the root causes of violence without the lens of white supremacy.

Talk to your friends and community members about how the media can influence our perceptions, and about how you can change the conversation so this biased influence stops spreading.

The six Black women and three Black men who lost their lives in Charleston were all inspirational models of leadership in their communities.

We can never get them back, and we can't erase the way the mainstream media failed them by misrepresenting the cause of their deaths.

But for them, for Sandra Bland, and for all of those who were killed or traumatized, only to be re-victimized by the media, we need to demand more respect for people of color.

> "*The American Psychological Association, citing a number of academic studies on the issue, adopted a resolution in 2014 recommending the immediate retirement of Native American mascots, images, symbols and personalities by schools, colleges, athletic teams and other organizations.*"

Native Americans are Stereotyped in the Media

Farah Qureshi

In the following viewpoint, Farah Qureshi argues that Native American advocacy groups have launched campaigns to eliminate harmful media portrayals such as using Native American mascots for sports teams. The advocacy groups find that sports team mascots are the only representations Native Americans see of themselves in the media. Recent research has shown that using these team mascots leads to poor self-esteem and mental health for Native American youth and contributes to cultural biases and prejudices. Farah Qureshi is a doctoral candidate in social and behavioral sciences at the Harvard School of Public Health.

"Native Americans: Negative Impacts of Media Portrayals, Stereotypes," Farah Qureshi, Journalist's Resource, February 10, 2016. http://journalistsresource.org/studies/society/race-society/native-americans-media-stereotype-redskins. Licensed under CC BY 3.0.

As you read, consider the following questions:

1. What has been the impact of Native American campaigns to eliminate cultural stereotypes in high school and professional sports?
2. According to the author, why has the American Psychological Association recommended the retirement of Native American mascots by schools and athletic teams?
3. What did the 2015 study on the media representation of Native Americans conclude about the impact of stereotypes on Native American youth?

Controversies around the continued use of Native American mascots for high schools and professional sports teams have reached a fever pitch in recent years, most notably with the U.S. Patent and Trademark Office's 2014 cancellation of six trademarks held by Washington's NFL team. The team is still trying to reverse the government agency's decision and a ruling is expected in 2016. Meanwhile, Native American advocacy groups such as the National Congress of American Indians have launched large-scale campaigns to eliminate harmful media portrayals and garner public support for changes. One example of those campaigns is Proud to Be: The Campaign to End Harmful Indian Mascots. While these movements typically cite history to support their cause, they also are bolstered by a body of research on the negative psychological effects of such portrayals on indigenous people. For instance, a 2014 report by the Center for American Progress suggests that using Native American mascots and team names results in poorer self-esteem and mental health for Native youth and also contributes to the development of cultural biases and prejudices. The American Psychological Association, citing a number of academic studies on the issue, adopted a resolution in 2014 recommending the immediate retirement of Native American mascots, images, symbols and personalities by schools, colleges, athletic teams and other organizations.

To get a better understanding of the impact of media representations, four scholars from four U.S. universities collaborated on a 2015 study that was published in the *Journal of Social Issues*. The authors are Peter A. Leavitt of the University of Arizona, Rebecca Covarrubias of the University of Delaware, Yvonne A. Perez of Syracuse University and Stephanie A. Fryberg of the University of Washington. Their study, titled "'Frozen in Time': The Impact of Native American Media Representations on Identity and Self-Understanding," looks at how mass media influences the way Native Americans see themselves and how others see and understand them. The authors examine the quality and quantity of how Native people are represented in the media, which includes news coverage, TV shows, films and video games.

Key points include:

- Native Americans experience "relative invisibility" in the media. When they are included, they generally are portrayed as historical figures "—individuals from the 18th and 19th centuries who wear buckskin, ride horses or live in teepees. When they are shown as modern people, they often are associated with addiction, poverty and a lack of formal education.
- When Native Americans are included in media depictions, they are usually shown as a particular type of Native American "—for example, as Sioux, Navajo or Apache. This narrow representation does not reflect the wide diversity among the hundreds of tribal cultures that exist within the borders of the United States.
- Native Americans make up a very small percentage of the U.S. population but are much underrepresented in the media. American Indians and Alaska Natives made up about 2 percent of the total population in 2013, according to the U.S. Census Bureau. The percentage of characters in popular films and primetime TV shows who are Native

American ranges from zero to 0.4 percent, according to content analyses. Less than 1 percent of children's cartoon characters are Native Americans, who make up 0.09 percent of video game characters.

- The lack of accurate representation is heightened by the fact that the average U.S. resident experiences nearly no direct, daily interaction with Native Americans. Only 14 states have American Indian populations that exceed 100,000 people. Nearly one-fourth of Native people live on reservations.
- Inaccurate and negative media depictions have psychological consequences. For example, exposure to common media portrayals has been shown to have a harmful impact on Native American high school students' feelings about themselves, their community and their academic possibilities.
- Media depictions of Native Americans can influence how Native people see themselves. Some may be motivated to identify with representations, even if they are inaccurate, "simply because one representation is better than no representation."

The authors note that the ideas presented in their study have widespread implications for public policy. As one example, the authors suggest that policy makers support making schools "free from limiting and negative representations that influence the future potential of Native American students." Another way to change how Native people are portrayed is by creating policies that require media outlets to consider how and when they represent minority groups.

> *"I struggled to get my students to address the 'elephant in the room'"—that the majority of the surrounding lower social class neighborhood comprised racial minorities, whereas the majority of my students and BSC professors, including myself, benefited from 'white privilege.'"*

We are Not a Color-blind Society

Meghan L. Mills

In the following viewpoint, Meghan L. Mills argues that many Americans feel as if the country has evolved into a "color-blind" society, where people's skin color doesn't matter. People have been socialized to not even discuss race because of the myth that the United States has moved into a post-race era. Some scholars see this perception as dangerous, because it prevents serious and meaningful discussion about problems caused by racism. Meghan L. Mills is assistant professor of sociology at Birmingham-Southern College.

As you read, consider the following questions:

1. How does the author define the concept of "color-blind racism?"
2. What does the author believe is the impact of refusing to discuss racism in the classroom?
3. Why does the author believe that color-blind racism is more dangerous than the racism during the Jim Crow period?

Following the recent events featured in the media such as the riots in Baltimore that came after the fatal shooting of Freddie Gray, Rachel Dolezal stepping down as the Spokane Washington NAACP president, and the tragic shootings in Charleston, South Carolina, public discussions have primarily focused on issues surrounding individual responsibility and mental illness.

I read these conversations with disappointment and frustration.

The dominant approach to understanding racial inequality in the US today is "color-blind racism." This is the belief that racial inequality can be attributed only to issues considered to be "race-neutral". In other words, because racial discrimination is now illegal, everyone is born with an equal opportunity to achieve the "American Dream," no matter their race.

In comparison to the overt and legal racism prior to the Civil Rights movement, this "new" transformed type of racism is seemingly invisible, making meaningful societal discussions near impossible, and in turn perpetuating racial inequality, which then expresses itself, as we have seen, in these recent incidents.

Conversations with students

What about classrooms? Are adequate conversations around race taking place in that space? And how can scholars shape some of the discussions?

A clear example of "color-blind racism" unexpectedly arose my first year as an assistant professor of sociology at Birmingham-Southern College (BSC) in Birmingham, Alabama.

Being a "Yankee," I was warned in advance that my students at BSC would be more politically and socially conservative than what I was used to (coming from the University of New Hampshire).

However, midway into my first semester, I found that the majority of my students were able to critically engage in potentially controversial topics such as LGBT rights, health care reform and the legalization of marijuana. We also discussed the class inequality between them as middle- or upper-class students living within the gated "hilltop" campus and the surrounding lower social class neighborhood immediately outside of the campus gates.

The real challenge arose when it came to discussing race in the classroom.

I struggled to get my students to address the "elephant in the room"—that the majority of the surrounding lower social class neighborhood comprised racial minorities, whereas the majority of my students and BSC professors, including myself, benefited from "white privilege," the often unacknowledged advantages with which whites are born, based solely on the color of their skin.

Challenges of talking about race

I had incorrectly assumed that teaching in Birmingham, Alabama, with its rich social and cultural history of the Civil Rights movement and racial heterogeneity, would make discussing racial inequality one of the most engaging and meaningful discussions in the course.

My students refused to discuss race beyond a superficial level.

I found the majority of my students, primarily from the South, have been "socialized" to not discuss race because "race doesn't matter" and we are (or should be) a "color-blind" society.

This was illustrated by student responses such as "there is only one race: human" and "only racists see race" when asked in class whether race still matters. The responses were consistently given by students across my four classes.

DISCRIMINATION CAN SOMETIMES MAKES SENSE

It can be proved that statistical discrimination is sometimes efficient. As an example, consider the well-known complaint that it's harder for African-Americans to catch a cab. This might be because taxi drivers are racist in sense, but I doubt it. More likely, taxi drivers are engaged in statistical discrimination. Cab driving is a rather dangerous business, because among patrons there are a few bad apples who might rob or even kill you. Doubtless, the vast majority of black taxi customers are law-abiding, but it is nonetheless a statistical fact that crime rates are higher among blacks, so the cab driver runs a greater risk. From an economist's point of view, a smart solution would be to allow cab drivers to practice statistical discrimination by charging black clients more! The higher price would compensate for the greater risk, and blacks would have just as easy a time catching a cab. By that logic, explicit racial price discrimination by cab drivers might make the world a better place. But we're unwilling to tolerate that, so cab drivers probably optimize by avoiding black clients. The somewhat serendipitous nature of customer-taxi contacts — Did he avoid me or did he just not see me hail him? — makes statistical discrimination difficult to regulate.

Conversations with several of my faculty colleagues across disciplines also revealed that this was a common theme.

What I learned was that in order to get students to more effectively discuss issues of race, I needed to first address one of the most dangerous social myths perpetuating racial inequality in today's society—that we are a "color-blind" society.

How to teach race

I have modified my lesson on race to begin, not end, with a discussion of "color-blind racism." What I have found to be most critical to this discussion is challenging my students to apply their "sociological imaginations," which can enable them to look at underlying social issues behind some recent news events.

As good sociologists-in-training, my students are asked to consider the larger social structural concerns (eg, poverty, institutional racism, the criminal justice system) instead of focusing on individuals (eg, Baltimore police officers, Rachael Dolezal, Dylann Roof).

My experiences in the classroom are by no means an isolated incident. Research consistently indicates this "color-blind" ideology permeates education, politics, the criminal justice system, the media, etc.

This "color-blind racism" is as dangerous as, if not more dangerous than, the overt racism during Jim Crow. It is for the most part invisible and easily overlooked in public discussions on social issues and therefore very effectively perpetuates racial inequality.

If the majority of my college students believe it is wrong to even "see" race, how can they be expected to meaningfully discuss larger issues of institutional racism and inequality? How can we as a society expect more meaningful social discussions and solutions?

As scholars, we need to emphasize to our students that race is a real thing, with real consequences. As long as we as a society continue avoiding "seeing" or meaningfully discussing race, we will continue to have Baltimore riots and Charleston shootings.

"*BLM claims inspiration from the African-American Civil Rights Movement, the Black Power movement, the 1980s Black feminist movement, Pan-Africanism, Anti-Apartheid Movement, Hip hop, LGBTQ social movements, and Occupy Wall Street.*"

Black Lives Matter is a Response to Racial Violence

Boundless

The following viewpoint examines the Black Lives Matter (BLM) movement in its campaigns against violence and institutionalized racism toward black Americans. It began in 2013 after the acquittal of George Zimmerman in the shooting death of Trayvon Martin. The additional deaths of Michael Brown in Ferguson, Missouri, Eric Garner in New York City, and Freddie Gray in Baltimore, Maryland, and others further galvanized the movement under the social media hashtag #BlackLivesMatter.

As you read, consider the following questions:

1. What events led up to the creation of the Black Lives Matter movement on social media?
2. What leadership roles did Black Lives Matter organizers take after additional deaths of black people at the hands of police became widely publicized?
3. How has the Black Lives Matter movement expanded in the years following the trial of George Zimmerman in 2013?

The Rise of Black Lives Matter

Black Lives Matter (BLM) is an activist movement, originating in the African-American community, that campaigns against violence and institutionalized racism toward black people in the United States. BLM regularly organizes protests around the deaths of black people in killings by law enforcement officers, as well as broader issues of racial profiling, police brutality, and racial inequality in the United States criminal justice system.

The movement began in 2013 with the use of the hashtag #BlackLivesMatter on social media, after the acquittal of George Zimmerman in the shooting death of African-American teen Trayvon Martin. Black Lives Matter became nationally recognized for its street demonstrations following the 2014 deaths of two African Americans: Michael Brown, resulting in protests and unrest in Ferguson, and Eric Garner in New York City.

Events 2012–Today

Trayvon Martin and the Acquittal of George Zimmerman

Trayvon Benjamin Martin was an African American from Miami Gardens, Florida, who, at 17 years old, was fatally shot by George Zimmerman, a neighborhood watch volunteer, in Sanford, Florida. On the evening of February 26, 2012, Martin had gone to a convenience store and purchased candy and a canned drink. As Martin returned from the store, he walked through a neighborhood that had been victimized by robberies several times that year. Zimmerman, a member of the community watch, spotted him and called the Sanford Police to report him for suspicious behavior. Moments later, Martin was shot in the chest. Zimmerman was not charged at the time of the shooting by the Sanford Police, who said that there was no evidence to refute his claim of self-defense and that Florida's stand your ground law prohibited law-enforcement officials from arresting or charging him. After national media focused on the tragedy, Zimmerman was eventually charged and tried in Martin's death. A jury acquitted Zimmerman of second-degree murder and of manslaughter in July 2013.

Michael Brown and Ferguson
Michael Brown, an 18-year-old black man, was shot and killed on August 9, 2014, in Ferguson, Missouri, by Darren Wilson, a 28-year-old white Ferguson police officer. The disputed circumstances of the shooting of the unarmed man sparked existing tensions in the predominantly black city, where protests and civil unrest erupted. The events received considerable attention in the U.S. and elsewhere, attracted protesters from outside the region, and sparked a vigorous debate in the United States about the relationship between law enforcement officers and African Americans, the militarization of the police, and the Use of Force Doctrine in Missouri and nationwide. Continued activism expanded the issues to include modern-day debtors prisons, for-profit policing, and school segregation.

As the details of the original shooting emerged, police established curfews and deployed riot squads to maintain order. Peaceful protests were met with police militarization, and some areas of the city turned violent. The unrest continued on November 24, 2014, after a grand jury did not indict Officer Wilson.

Eric Garner
On July 17, 2014, Eric Garner, a 43-year-old African American man, was killed in Staten Island, New York City, after a New York City Police Department (NYPD) officer put him in what has been

described as a chokehold for about 15 to 19 seconds while arresting him for allegedly selling cigarettes, which Garner had denied. The New York City Medical Examiner's Office attributed Garner's death to a combination of a chokchold, compression of his chest, and poor health. NYPD policy prohibits the use of chokeholds, and video shows Garner repeatedly telling the officer "I can't breathe" before he lost consciousness. The medical examiner ruled Garner's death a homicide.

On December 3, 2014, the Richmond County grand jury decided not to indict Officer Pantaleo, who had performed the chokehold. On that day, the United States Department of Justice announced it would conduct an independent investigation. The event stirred public protests and rallies, with charges of police brutality made by protesters. By December 28, 2014, at least 50 demonstrations had been held nationwide specifically for Garner, while hundreds of demonstrations against general police brutality counted Garner as a focal point. On July 13, 2015, an out-of-court settlement was announced in which the City of New York would pay the Garner family $5.9 million.

Freddie Gray and Baltimore Protests

On April 12, 2015, Baltimore Police Department officers arrested Freddie Gray, a 25-year-old African American resident of Baltimore, Maryland, for possessing what the police alleged was an illegal switchblade. Gray sustained heavy injuries to his neck and spine while in transport in a police vehicle and fell into a coma. On April 18, 2015, the residents of Baltimore protested in front of the Western district police station. Gray died the following day, April 19, 2015, a week after the arrest. On April 21, 2015, pending an investigation of the incident, six Baltimore police officers were suspended with pay.

Further protests were organized after Gray's death became public knowledge, amid the police department's continuing inability to adequately or consistently explain the events following the arrest and the injuries. Spontaneous protests started after the funeral service, and civil unrest continued with at least 250 people arrested, at least 20 police officers injured, 285 to 350 businesses damaged, 60 structure fires, thousands of police and Maryland National Guard troops deployed, and a state of emergency declared in the city limits of Baltimore. On May 1, 2015, Gray's death was ruled to be a homicide, and legal charges were issued against the six officers involved in the incident, including that of second-degree murder. The state of emergency was lifted on May 6.

In September 2015, it was decided that there would be separate trials for the accused officers. The first trial against Officer William Porter ended in mistrial in December 2015. Officer Edward Nero subsequently opted for a bench trial and was found not guilty by Circuit Judge Barry William in May 2016. In June, Officer Caesar Goodson, who faced the most severe charges, was also acquitted by Williams by means of a bench trial.

Organizing Against Violence

The Black Lives Matter movement was co-founded by three black queer women who are active community organizers: Alicia Garza, Patrisse Cullors, and Opal Tometi. BLM claims inspiration from the African-American Civil Rights Movement, the Black Power movement, the 1980s Black feminist movement, Pan-Africanism, Anti-Apartheid Movement, Hip hop, LGBTQ social movements, and Occupy Wall Street. Garza, Cullors and Tometi met through "Black Organizing for Leadership & Dignity" (BOLD), a national organization that trains community organizers. They began to question how they were going to respond to the devaluation of black lives after Zimmerman's acquittal. Garza wrote a Facebook post titled "A Love Note to Black People" in which she wrote: "Our Lives Matter, Black Lives Matter." Cullors replied: "#BlackLivesMatter." Tometi then added her support, and Black Lives Matter was born as an online campaign.

Periodical and Internet Sources Bibliography

The following articles have been selected to supplement the diverse views presented in this chapter.

John Blake, "It's Time to Talk About 'Black Privilege,'" *CNN*, March 31, 2016.

Sam Fulwood III, "Race and Beyond: The Media's Stereotypical Portrayals of Race," Center for American Progress, March 5, 2013.

Jon Greenberg, "7 Reasons Why 'Colorblindness' Contributes to Racism Instead of Solves It," *Everyday Feminism,* February 23, 2015.

Jackelyn Hwang, "Gentrification without Segregation: Race and Renewal in a Diversifying City," Harvard Joint Center for Housing Studies, May 2016.

National Congress of American Indians, "Ending the Era of Harmful 'Indian' Mascots," 2016.

National Hispanic Media Coalition, "The Impact of Media Stereotypes on Opinions and Attitudes Towards Latinos," 2016.

Pew Research Center, "On Views of Race and Inequality, Blacks and Whites are Worlds Apart," June 27, 2016.

Richard Prince, "How Media Have Shaped Our Perception of Race and Crime," *Root*, September 4, 2014.

Fiona Teng, "Guide to Getting Uncomfortable with Race," *Huffington Post*, December 11, 2015.

Wendy Wang, "The Rise of Intermarriage," Pew Research Center, Feb. 16, 2012

Adia Harvey Wingfield, "Color-Blindness is Counterproductive," *Atlantic*, September 13, 2015.

OPPOSING VIEWPOINTS® SERIES

| Is Justice Color-Blind?

Chapter Preface

When Barack Obama began his presidency in 2008, many people were optimistic that the country could finally address the issues of race in rational and productive ways. Perhaps, many hoped, discussions in the White House and Congress would focus on the myriad ways race intersected with problems in education, housing, employment, health care, and immigration. Instead, seven months into Obama's first administration, the nation received the first of a long list of lessons about the role of race in the criminal justice system.

Harvard history professor Henry Louis Gates Jr., who is African-American, was arrested for breaking into his own home by a white police officer. Though charges were eventually dropped, the high-profile incident caught the attention of President Obama, who invited Professor Gates and arresting officer Sergeant James Crowley to the White House for a conciliatory meeting. To many, the arrest represented evidence of racism and racial profiling that they thought was endemic in most law enforcement agencies in the United States.

Those who think that criminal justice systems in the United States are not color-blind have statistics to back them up. Racial discrepancies begin early. US Department of Education data shows that black students account for 18 percent of the country's pre-K enrollment, but made up 48 percent of school suspensions. There are racial disparities in in a variety of law enforcement issues, such as traffic stops, arrests for marijuana, sentencing for cocaine felonies, and men on death row.

The reasons for racial discrepancies in the criminal justice system are complex. Many black communities are plagued by issues such as poverty, disrupted families, high numbers of unemployed ex-cons, and struggling schools. Teens in these neighborhoods often accumulate a record of low-level arrests, leading to tougher sentences when they commit felonies. In addition, the US Justice

Department has documented cases of systematic racism in police departments and criminal court systems. State and federal prison systems are still coping with the devastating effects of the failed war on drugs in the 1980s and '90s.

While experts debate the causes of high rates of black arrest and incarceration, many criminal justice professionals agree that solutions to these problems will be found in the wider communities where people of color live, go to school, and work. Addressing disparities in education, health care, housing, and employment opportunities can reduce the conditions that breed criminal behavior. Equally important is consistent and high quality training in law enforcement to root out and eliminate racism. The articles in this chapter address these issues in sometimes personal ways, allowing readers to find their own answers to the question: Is the US justice system color-blind?

> *"That report showed that while black children represent 18 percent of preschool enrollment, they accounted for 48 percent of students receiving one or more suspensions."*

Inequality in Justice Begins Early

Esther Canty-Barnes

In the following viewpoint, Esther Canty-Barnes argues that recent research shows that minority children are disciplined or expelled from school at rates several times higher than white students. Because of poverty or early trauma, many minority students display acting-out behaviors that are not adequately addressed. In other cases minority students are disciplined for minor behaviors that are overlooked in white students. These negative experiences can have long-lasting effects on the progress of many students. Esther Canty-Barnes is clinical professor of law and director of the Education and Health Law Clinic at Rutgers University Newark.

As you read, consider the following questions:

1. According to the author, what are some of the root causes of behaviors that lead to school suspensions or expulsions?

2. What does the author mean by school districts "criminalizing and dehumanizing" vulnerable children.

3. What is the impact of school suspensions both on the children involved and the communities in which they live?

On Wednesday, July 6, the four-year-old daughter of Diamond Reynolds witnessed the killing of Philando Castile by a Minnesota police officer. She and her mother sat in close proximity to Castile when he was shot.

A 2009 Department of Justice study showed that more than 60 percent of American children had directly or indirectly been exposed to violence within the past year. Exposure to such violence has long-term physical, psychological and emotional implications.

When these children enter school, they have unique needs. Many are ill-prepared for the social, emotional and academic rigor that is anticipated and required. Conversely, many schools are not prepared to handle the needs of children who have been victims of poverty, trauma or who have special education needs.

Preschool experience could help prepare children for learning in academic, social and emotional spheres of elementary education. In my role as a clinical professor of law and director of the Education and Health Law Clinic at Rutgers Law School, it is not uncommon for me to represent parents of young children who have been suspended or have had a history of being suspended as early as preschool or kindergarten.

Preschool Suspensions and Black Kids

For the first time in March 2014, the U.S. Department of Education, Office of Civil Rights (OCR) collected data regarding how early learners are disciplined during the 2011–12 school year.

That report showed that while black children represent 18 percent of preschool enrollment, they accounted for 48 percent of students receiving one or more suspensions. White children, on the other hand, represented over 40 percent of the total enrollment, but a little more than 25 percent of such suspensions.

A suspension involves the removal of a student from school for violations of a school's code of conduct for one or more days. These violations could vary depending on the state and local school district policies. They could include infractions such as tardiness, dress code violations, failure to follow directions and "willful disobedience." In public schools, short-term suspensions typically are 10 days or less. More than 10 consecutive days of suspension require greater due process rights.

A March 2016 OCR report shows a continuation of the disturbing trends and disparities of the 2014 report. This time, the OCR provided more data by breaking down preschool suspension rates based upon race and gender. For the 2013-14 year, the report shows that black children attending public preschools were 3.6 times more likely to receive one or more suspensions compared to their white counterparts.

According to the 2016 OCR report, black boys were at greater risk for preschool suspensions. Even though preschool boys represented almost 20 percent of enrolled preschoolers, they represented 45 percent of male students receiving one or more out-of-school suspensions. Even more problematic were the statistics for black girls. Although they represented 20 percent of female preschool enrollment, they accounted for over 50 percent of female students with one or more out of school suspensions.

A national pre-kindergarten study conducted in 2005 identified similar disparities with respect to these vulnerable children. That study, conducted by Walter S. Gilliam at Yale University, concluded that preschool children were expelled at a rate of more than three times that of students in K-12.

According to the same report, African-American children attending state-funded preschools were about twice as likely to be expelled as Latino and Caucasian children.

More than 10 years have passed since this study, and the problem still persists.

Why Are Kids Suspended?

The root causes of suspensions and expulsions of early learners vary. An overwhelming majority focus on behavior.

Studies have differed on the causes of behaviors that lead to suspension of children.

These vary from lack of prenatal and maternal care, poverty, exposure to trauma and harsh discipline practices to language disorders and disability-related diagnoses.

Children born into poverty lack exposure to educational experiences that would prepare them to enter a formal school setting. African-Americans and American Indian children are about three times as likely to live in poverty as their white counterparts. About half had no parent with full-time employment. Latino families also had high rates of poverty, at 32 percent.

Environmental issues such as exposure to lead and toxins could also play an important role.

Less tolerant and discriminatory treatment based on race could also be a factor. In such instances, black children are viewed as more mature and less innocent than their white counterparts. They are removed from school for minor infractions.

Often, these children may suffer from neurological, psychological, learning or medically based disabilities. However, based on my experience, these factors are not always considered or identified in a timely manner.

School Environment Through K-12

Suspensions at the preschool level are the tip of the iceberg. Black and brown students continue to be suspended disproportionately at the elementary and secondary levels.

The media is full of examples of black children being suspended, handcuffed or arrested by police at a young age. For instance, a six-year-old girl in Georgia was handcuffed and taken to the police station for throwing a tantrum and destroying school property. A seven-year-old with Attention Deficit Disorder was handcuffed for acting out, and a six-year-old Florida girl was handcuffed and sent to a mental institution for hitting the school principal. The manner in which these children were treated is not characteristic of nurturing or caring school environments.

According to OCR's 2016 report, of the 2.8 million K-12 students receiving one or more suspensions, 1.1 million were black; 600,000 were Latino; 660,000 were disabled; and 210,000 were English language learners.

School districts have criminalized and dehumanized very vulnerable children for minor school infractions, such as talking back to the teacher or not wearing a school uniform. A blatant example of this draconian behavior occurred in Meridian, Mississippi where small infractions led to the arrest, confinement and conviction of students in what was characterized by the Department of Justice as a "school-to-prison-pipeline." Some of these children were as young as 10.

The Meridian School District referred students to the Police Department for small infractions. All students referred were handcuffed, arrested and sent to the County juvenile justice system without consideration of their rights to due process or representation by an attorney at all stages of the process.

Against the Law

Federal laws prohibit such discrimination. Special Education laws also prohibit school districts from suspending and expelling students with disabilities without providing procedural protections.

In fact, a joint policy letter, issued in 2014 by the the U.S. Departments of Health and Human Services and Education, strongly urged early child care providers to establish policies and procedures aimed at eliminating the suspension of preschoolers.

But intentionally or unintentionally, these laws or policies are often overlooked or blatantly ignored.

Some states and local school districts are taking action to address this problem. States such as Arkansas, Colorado, Maryland and Oregon have passed bills focused on improving outcomes and addressing the disproportionate suspension of students of color.

But much more needs to be done to address this issue. Young students are still pushed out and suspended. In fact, by the time some children reach first grade, they may have had several negative school experiences.

Repairing Broken Men is Harder

The problem that many schools face is a lack of resources attributable to a lack of funding. Unfortunately, sometimes, students are suspended because schools lack the resources to address their specific and unique needs.

In contrast to the decrease in funds in education, the funding for the prison industry has increased geometrically.

Children who are suspended or expelled from school at such an early age have a greater risk for dropping out of school and entering the juvenile justice or prison system.

When children are suspended for substantial periods of time, it becomes a more difficult task to keep up with school work and to catch up once he or she returns to school. There is no positive rationale for the degree to which zero tolerance policies have been used.

For the cost of incarcerating a juvenile in some states, a child could receive a quality private school college education.

A quote by Frederick Douglass, an abolitionist born into slavery, is still appropriate today.

"It is easier to build strong children than to repair broken men."

"At the height of America's war on drugs, from the 1980s through the mid-2000s, more than 20 prisons opened in California, compared with just 12 between 1852 and 1984."

Black Drug Offenders Are More Likely to Go To Jail

Saki Knafo

In the following viewpoint, Saki Knafo examines a proposal under consideration by the California state legislature that would have addressed the disproportionate incarceration of black people for drug offenses. Black adults are arrested at higher rates and incarcerated for longer periods than white adults, which often leads to unemployment, denial of public housing, and loss of student financial aid. The bill, which was eventually vetoed by Governor Jerry Brown, would also have relieved the high budget demands of maintaining one of the country's largest prison systems. Saki Knafo has written for the New York Times Magazine, New York, *the* Believer, GQ, Details, *and* Publishers Weekly.

"When It Comes to Illegal Drug Use, White American Does the Crime, Black America Gets the Time," Saki Knafo, Huffington Post, September 18, 2013. Reprinted by permission.

As you read, consider the following questions:

1. According to the author, why are black Californians arrested at higher rates than white Californians for drug offenses?
2. According to the author, what impact does incarceration have on those people convicted of a felony offense after they serve their term?
3. What would California SB 649 do for those arrested for drug offenses?

White Americans are more likely than black Americans to have used most kinds of illegal drugs, including cocaine, marijuana and LSD. Yet blacks are far more likely to go to prison for drug offenses.

This discrepancy forms the backdrop of a new legislative proposal in California, which aims to reduce the disproportionate incarceration of black people in the state. Supporters of the bill, SB 649, point to some striking national data.

Nearly 20 percent of whites have used cocaine, compared with 10 percent of blacks and Latinos, according to a 2011 survey from the Substance Abuse and Mental Health Services Administration— the most recent data available.

Higher percentages of whites have also tried hallucinogens, marijuana, pain relievers like OxyContin, and stimulants like methamphetamine, according to the survey. Crack is more popular among blacks than whites, but not by much.

Still, blacks are arrested for drug possession more than three times as often as whites, according to a 2009 report from the advocacy group Human Rights Watch.

Of the 225,242 people who were serving time in state prisons for drug offenses in 2011, blacks made up 45 percent and whites comprised just 30 percent, according to the Bureau of Justice Statistics.

New Legislation Can Reduce Mass Incarceration

In spite of signature 1960s legislation intended to eradicate systemic racism from the political, social, and economic spheres, there are still structures in place that perpetuate unjust treatment and inequality within our society. One of the best examples can be found in the criminal justice system.

[…]

The proposed Smarter Sentencing Act of 2015 (S.502/H.R.920), introduced by a bipartisan group of lawmakers including Senators Mike Lee and Dick Durbin and Representatives Raul Labrador and Bobby Scott, would have a multitude of beneficial impacts on the criminal justice system. First, it would allow the Fair Sentencing Act to be applied retroactively, making thousands of convicts eligible for sentencing reviews. In addition, the bill would restrict the use of mandatory-minimum sentencing rules that require lengthy prison terms regardless of the circumstances in a given case. Though this bill enjoys broad support ranging from fiscal conservatives to staunch liberals, its proponents face an uphill battle. Most of those opposing the measure are conservatives of the "tough on crime" school. Members of Congress and others who favor fundamental fairness should be putting their weight behind this bill, while also noting the secondary benefit of reducing the costs of mass incarceration.

"Calling for Progress: Racial Inequality and Criminal Justice Reform," Andrew Oravecz, Freedom House, October 15, 2015.

Jamie Fellner, author of the Human Rights Watch report, offered an explanation for this discrepancy.

"The race issue isn't just that the judge is going, 'Oh, black man, I'm gonna sentence you higher,'" she said. "The police go into low-income minority neighborhoods and that's where they make most of their drug arrests. If they arrest you, now you have a 'prior,' so if you plead or get arrested again, you're gonna have a higher sentence. There's a kind of cumulative effect."

Lawmakers in California hope to blunt that effect. Last week, both houses of the state legislature passed SB 649, which would give judges and prosecutors the option of charging people convicted of drug offenses with misdemeanors instead of felonies. Those offenders could then be sent to substance abuse treatment centers instead of prison or jail.

Supporters of the bill, including its author, state Sen. Mark Leno (D-San Francisco), note that black adults represent one-quarter of all felony drug arrests in California, despite comprising just 5 percent of the state population.

"One can take it to conspiratorial or racist theories or not," Leno told HuffPost. "The motivation I don't think needs to be determined. The results are the same: Our policy and lawmaking perpetuate a chronic underclass of citizens."

Former prisoners who were convicted of felonies often face steep official barriers to "the very things that are needed to keep one successful in recovery," he added—namely, education, housing and employment.

The federal government can deny public housing assistance to anyone who has been convicted of a felony drug offense. Students who have been convicted of drug possession are barred from receiving federal financial aid and substantial education tax credits. And employers often require applicants to disclose their criminal histories, despite a growing nationwide movement to ban that practice.

Not all drug offenses in California automatically result in felony charges. Methamphetamine, LSD and certain other drugs are known as "wobblers," meaning that possession of those drugs can be charged as a felony or a misdemeanor. The new bill would basically extend this "wobbler" approach to heroin, cocaine and most other drugs. Blacks use heroin and cocaine more than they use meth and LSD, which are primarily used by whites.

In recent years, states from New York to Texas have adopted reforms that resemble SB 649, and leaders across the political spectrum have pushed for changes to the country's drug sentencing policies. In August, Attorney General Eric Holder announced that the Justice Department would no longer pursue mandatory minimum sentences for certain low-level drug offenders, citing "shameful" racial disparities in the criminal justice system.

Yet some drug reform advocates worry that Gov. Jerry Brown (D) might not sign the California measure, noting that he has often seemed reluctant to embrace progressive criminal justice policies.

Like other reforms aimed at reducing California's prison population, SB 649 could help relieve the state's budgetary woes, supporters say. Drug sentencing policies are widely blamed for the enormous size and costs of the country's prison systems. And few prison systems are bigger or more expensive than California's.

At the height of America's war on drugs, from the 1980s through the mid-2000s, more than 20 prisons opened in California, compared with just 12 between 1852 and 1984. California's prison population increased more than fivefold in the later decades, and prisons now cost the state's taxpayers close to $10 billion a year.

> "*Ultimately, the best way to reduce the collateral consequences and the criminogenic effects of high rates of incarceration and their subsequent negative effects for communities of color is to reduce the number of people going into prisons and to create a more just society.*"

Mass Incarcerations are Damaging Neighborhoods

Robert D. Crutchfield and Gregory A. Weeks

In the following viewpoint, Robert Crutchfield and Gregory Weeks argue that in disadvantaged communities, there is a tipping point at which crime policies can do more harm than good. Mass incarcerations of people of color disrupt families and undermine community stability, which can later increase crime. Large numbers of convicted felons returning to old neighborhoods often do not find treatment for drug issues, employment, or intact families or supportive communities. Robert D. Crutchfield is a professor in the department of sociology at the University of Washington. Gregory A. Weeks is a retired judge for the Fourth Division of the Superior Court of North Carolina.

Reprinted with permission from *Issues in Science and Technology*, Crutchfield and Weeks, "The Effects of Mass Incarceration on Communities of Color," Fall 2015, pp. 46-51, by the University of Texas at Dallas, Richardson, TX.

As you read, consider the following questions:

1. What do the authors mean by the "collateral damages" that families of those imprisoned receive?
2. According to the authors, how does incarcerating too many residents of one neighborhood actually increase the crime rate?
3. What have the authors discovered about the "unintended consequences" of high rates of incarceration in particular neighborhoods?

Understandably, most of us would expect that removing criminals—those who would victimize others—from a community would be welcomed by the populace, and that both residents and their property would be better off as a result. For most places, that is likely true. Removing a person who has hurt others or who does not respect the property of others is tantamount to removing a thorn from a tender foot. But there is a growing body of evidence that suggests that this may not always be the case, because of the effects that time in prison has on individuals and their home communities. There are collateral consequences that accrue to imprisoned people even after their sentences are completed, and some criminologists believe that when the number of felons removed from a community is "too high," it may actually harm the places where they used to live. And, since most people who are incarcerated return to the same neighborhoods, or very similar places as those they were removed from, their presence in large numbers, when they go home, adds a substantial burden there, too.

Although the United States has made some progress, it remains a substantially racially segregated nation residentially. And, the country stays very economically segregated as well. It is not surprising that poor people of color have been incarcerated disproportionately during the massive increase in imprisonment that has occurred in the nation since the early 1980s. It is from poor communities of color that a very large number of felons are removed, and to these same neighborhoods that they return when their sentences end. This population churning has been called "coercive mobility" by criminologists. Although it is the intent of legislatures, judges, police, and prosecutors to protect citizens and communities, there is reason to believe that coercive mobility has the unintended consequence of actually increasing crime and victimization.

Some of the changes during this period of increased incarceration that disadvantaged people of color coming into the justice system were implemented with the help and support of African American political leadership, with the express purpose of protecting black and brown communities. Perhaps the best example of this is the initial federal sentences for crack cocaine offenses: conviction for crack selling (more heavily sold and used by people of color) resulting in a sentence 100 times more severe than for selling the same amount of powder cocaine (more heavily sold and used by whites).

A long-running academic debate among criminologists has gone on during this same period about race and justice, the central question being how much of high minority incarceration is a consequence of differential involvement in criminal behavior versus a biased criminal justice system. That debate is not settled. But one factor is pretty much agreed upon: There is overrepresentation of minority group members among those engaging in crime, but even after this is taken into account, people of color are overrepresented in U.S. prisons and jails. The question is how much of the high levels of incarceration of African Americans and Latinos is warranted by higher levels of crime and what proportion is unwarranted. The best research indicates that the answers to these questions should be answered by looking specifically at types of crimes. Among the most serious violent crimes, the evidence suggests that unwarranted racial disparity is modest. For less serious crimes, the proportion of unwarranted racial disparity increases. This can be seen clearly by considering the evidence on drug imprisonments resulting from the war on drugs. Good evidence indicates that racial and ethnic groups use and sell drugs proportionally to their representation in the population; so about 13 percent of drug users and sellers are African Americans, about 17 percent are from the various Latino groups, and approximately 65 percent are whites (whites tend to sell to whites; blacks to blacks). But, more than 50 percent of those imprisoned for drug sales or possession are people of color. In fact, one study by the group Human Rights Watch found that black men are sentenced on drug charges at a rate that is more than 13 times higher than white men.

Some observers have claimed that African American and Latino drug dealers are more likely to be arrested because their activities are more likely to occur in open air public drug markets than does the dealing of whites. But at least one study has found that police elect to pursue open air drug markets with minority dealers and ignore those where whites are selling. Overall, the war on drugs has been especially hard on minority individuals and communities, and this cannot be justified by overrepresentation of these groups in this particular form of criminal behavior.

Contrary to what some casual observers might think, residents of African American and Latino communities want crime control, as well as effective and fair policing and a criminal justice system that removes crime perpetrators but that is also accountable to those communities. Popular media reports that focus on the "don't snitch" norm of some segments of those communities mask important distinctions. First, the belief that a don't snitch mindset exists in black communities tends to "criminalize" the entire population. This feeds into the historical experience of many law abiding citizens living in these communities that as far as "the system" is concerned, they are all criminals. Most people living in communities of color are law abiding citizens who have little in the way of other housing options. They feel that they are stopped, hassled, and disrespected by police just as often as those who are actually committing crimes. For these folks, there is little incentive to cooperate with a system they believe will ultimately abandon them when a case is over. Second, people in these communities have to live there 24 hours a day, seven days a week. They know that law enforcement won't be there to protect them forever. They have to live with the very real fear of retaliation from criminals in the community if they cooperate. It is not unusual for witnesses, and even victims, to a crime to refuse to testify or cooperate because they believe that the system will abandon them when a case is over. To the extent that a don't snitch norm exists, it is primarily observed among some young people in very socially and economically disadvantaged communities. Also, the populations in even the most disadvantaged sections of cities are very heterogeneous with respect to views of police and criminal justice agencies and institutions. Young African Americans who wear "don't snitch" t-shirts are no more representative of their communities than young whites with multiple piercings and tattoos are of theirs.

Some observers perceive the "black lives matter" movement to include a demand to remove police from black neighborhoods. Nothing could be further from the truth. That movement is calling for effective and accountable policing. So when serious criminals—those who victimize and terrorize black and brown communities—are arrested, convicted, and imprisoned, there are multiple responses in the places where they lived and, more often than not, engaged in their predatory behavior. There may be those who see and lament "another brother oppressed by the man," but the vast majority of people who live there will be pleased that someone who hurt and victimized others is, at least for a time, no longer roaming their streets free to wreak more havoc.

Problems with the "solutions"

As is the case for every community, when criminals are removed from socially and economically disadvantaged African American and Latino communities, there is a benefit to those places. Not only is a person who would victimize others not able to do so, but crime, especially high levels of crime, are bad for the collective good of communities. Crime can destabilize neighborhoods. When people live in fear of personal or property victimization, they view their environment as a threatening, scary place. Such spaces do not promote the kind of cohesion and closeness among neighbors that is important for healthy and productive social engagement. When residential areas, and even commercial districts, are cohesive and individuals are engaged with each other, people can participate in the kinds of social life that make crime less likely. So, too much crime actually increases the likelihood of more crime.

What some criminologists fear is that going too far in the opposite direction—with the criminal justice system removing too many residents from a neighborhood—potentially causes two separate but related types of problems. With incarceration there is collateral damage to those locked up, as well as to those who they are connected to: partners, children, extended family, and any positive friendship networks they had. Also, and perhaps less obvious, removing too many people from a troubled neighborhood can have a detrimental, crime-causing effect.

The overwhelming majority of inmates will be released from prison after serving their sentences, and the nation has struggled with how to help them reenter society. Generally, released prisoners must return to the county where they last lived, which, for most, means returning to a poor and socially isolated inner-city neighborhood or community. The unprecedented numbers now being released have compounded the problem. Many prisoners entered the system with drug, alcohol, or mental problems. In the vast majority of instances, they received little or no treatment or counseling during their incarceration because of reduced funding for rehabilitation programs as well as the closing or scaling back of state mental facilities. Prisons, and even jails, have become the dumping grounds of necessity for those who have mental health issues. On another level, general health care within prisons, including mental health care, has been woefully inadequate, resulting in a number of lawsuits against both federal and state corrections systems. Unfortunately, this means that prisoners released back into their old communities return no better off—or, in many instances, worse off—than they were before being incarcerated.

In addition, released prisoners face collateral consequences that they were largely unaware of at the time they were originally sentenced. Collateral consequences to the imprisoned are the effects that remain after the formal sentence has been served. These damages are inflicted by law and by social practice. Among the former, some of the more onerous consequences are the legal denial of some social benefits—public housing access, welfare benefits, some college loans and grants, the right to vote, the right to live or work in certain places (school zones for some offenders), and requirements to register with local authorities. These damages were enacted by legislative bodies to punish those convicted of crimes, in the belief that those who violate "the social contract" should not benefit from the public's largess, or in the belief that barring convicted felons from some of the things that others have access to is for the good of the broader community. But, not having access to these "privileges" will inhibit some who have been released from prison from taking the straight, narrow, and legitimate path, and thus increase the likelihood of them becoming again involved in criminal behavior. In addition to legally specified collateral consequences of felony convictions (and in some jurisdictions some misdemeanor convictions), there are informal consequences as well. Those who are convicted frequently lose intimate relationships with partners or access to their children, and they are less likely to find employment. Significantly, these consequences accrue even among inmates who do not spend long sentences in "the big house."

There are also collateral damages to the families of those imprisoned, both while they are locked up and when they are released. One study, for example, found that the financial and time strain on the wives and girlfriends of inmates in upstate New York prisons imperiled relationships with both the women in prisoners' lives and their children. Since families are a good anchor for prisoners when they are released, disruptions in family life increase the chances of recidivism. Another study comparing neighborhoods with high and low rates of incarceration, found that in the former, the gender ratio is sufficiently thrown off by the number of men going into and coming out of prison that marriage markets are negatively affected.

It has long been known that adding too many new residents to cities and neighborhoods can have a "criminogenic" effect, because when there are more new faces, when there are ever changing faces, the integration of new arrivals into the community is inhibited, allowing greater individual anonymity. Such circumstances create fertile ground for crime to occur and perhaps flourish. To be clear, this does not mean that migrants bring crime with them. In fact, the evidence has long suggested that movers have less of the characteristics that are predictive of criminal behavior. The problem is the lack of social integration. Similarly, when communities lose too large of a segment of their population, this same important, crime-inhibiting social integration can be disrupted. It is important to remember that even people who break the law occupy many different roles. They are husbands or wives or girlfriends or boyfriends, sons, daughters, friends, coworkers, and neighbors. Families and the neighborhoods in which they reside struggle to fill the void when members are no longer there. The removal of too many people from communities can be disruptive. The nation has seen this in recent years when sections of formerly industrial capitals, such as Detroit, Cleveland, St. Louis, and Pittsburgh, have lost population as people left in search of jobs. Some criminologists believe that when people from a community are imprisoned at a high enough number—coercive mobility—the effect may also be criminogenic.

So there are two countervailing forces or arguments: that removing problem criminal people improves the life of neighborhoods, and that removing too many people and then returning them can be criminogenic. The two most prominent researchers who have made the case regarding coercive mobility and its deleterious effects are Dina Rose and Todd Clear. They believe that there is a tipping point, below which imprisonment is normally good for a community, but above which it becomes criminogenic. This effect, coercive mobility leading to crime, is not thought to happen everywhere, but in severely socially and economically disadvantaged places. This is, in part, because a large amount of serious crime occurs there, but also because such places have very limited resources and do not have the collective resiliency to overcome high levels of imprisonment and large numbers of released men and women returning to the same problematic neighborhoods from which they came, or ones very much like them.

Before considering the evidence for coercive mobility's effects on communities, one more very important negative force should be highlighted: the diminished state—human capital, in the words of sociologists—of most returning former prisoners. It is generally accepted that having a good, solid family life lowers the probability of a person becoming involved in crime, and that having employment (especially good employment) does the same. Predictably, those most likely to be sentenced to a term in prison are less likely than others of their age, race, and gender to be involved in a stable relationship or to have been employed in a high-quality job prior to their incarceration. When men and women return from prison, their family life has an even higher likelihood of having been disrupted, and their competitiveness on the job market is even more diminished than it was before they were incarcerated. Time in prison means that these already marginal people are more marginalized, and they tend to return to living in neighborhoods that are already distressed by the presence of too many disrupted families and high levels of joblessness. They add to the already overcrowded pool of residents likely to not be in good relationships, to not be good prospects as mates, and to be not competitive for the desirable good jobs that will help them stay out of jail or prison and might help their community's dismal economic state.

Which brings things back to the coercive mobility argument, as it may be critically important. If its proponents are correct, the very effort to reduce crime in some of the nation's highest crime communities is doing the opposite in the context of mass incarceration. As a consequence, the National Research Council (NRC) committee charged with studying the causes and consequences of high rates of imprisonment took some time to evaluate the evidence for and against this thesis. The evidence is not conclusive, but it is suggestive. As observed in cities across the country, incarceration is very concentrated geographically.

In addition, the evidence indicates that, indeed, the places that released prisoners return to are just as geographically concentrated in other ways, as shown by comparison of the racial and ethnic composition of high-incarceration neighborhoods with the rest of the city, and the poverty rates for these communities and the city as a whole. The areas of concentrated incarceration are in predominately minority districts. This is the case in cities throughout the United States. The committee also found strong evidence that these places are among the most economically and socially disadvantaged sections of U.S. cities.

Thus, there is little doubt about this portion of the argument: prisoners come from and return to a narrow group of neighborhoods, very disadvantaged ones. Two other aspects of the coercive mobility argument are less clear.

First, there is some evidence that this concentration pattern is criminogenic, but other researchers have not found evidence that this pattern increases crime above and beyond what would generally be expected for similar neighborhoods. The strongest evidence for the argument has been presented by Rose and Clear in "Incarceration, Social Capital and Crime: Examining the Unintended Consequences of Incarceration," based on their work in Tallahassee, Florida, and published in the journal *Criminology* in 1998, and in Clear's review of research in his book *Imprisoning Communities*, published in 2007. Some additional research has also provided support. The strongest evidence to the contrary comes from several studies conducted by James Lynch and William Sabol in Baltimore, which yielded mixed evidence, but could not confirm the idea that incarceration was increasing crime rates in some of the city's neighborhoods.

Second, critical to this notion is that there is a tipping point below which incarceration benefits communities, but above which high levels of coercive mobility increases crime rates. The research evidence does indicate that there is a nonlinear relationship between imprisonment and crime, which suggests that there is such a tipping point, but criminologists to date have not been able to settle on where that tipping point is.

After considering the evidence, the NRC committee concluded that it did not allow for affirmation that high levels of imprisonment cause crime in these neighborhoods. Interestingly, the committee reported that an analytically major problem for examining this thesis is that it is too hard—indeed, virtually impossible—to find enough white neighborhoods with the same levels of either imprisonment or disadvantage that exists routinely in many African American communities in nearly every major American city to allow for meaningful analysis. Cities in the United States are still far too racially segregated to make the analytic comparisons that are necessary, and the minority neighborhoods are where the disadvantaged are concentrated and from where prisoners are disproportionally drawn. So, although the committee could not affirm that high levels of incarceration increases crime in disadvantaged minority neighborhoods, it did find that the quantitative evidence is suggestive of that pattern. And a number of ethnographers—who have been spending time in these communities and watching how families, friendship networks, and communities are faring—are adding additional evidence that indicates that high levels of imprisonment, concentrated in disadvantaged communities of color, are indeed criminogenic.

Researchers are increasingly finding that both the collateral consequences of imprisonment, and living in communities from which many of the imprisoned come from and return to, do have detrimental effects. And these effects are visited upon the reentering individual, on their families, and on the communities at large. Reentering former inmates' chances of success and reduced probability of recidivism are enhanced if they are returning to healthy families and can find decent employment. It has been well established that men, whether or not they have been to prison, are less likely to be involved in crime if they are in stable intimate relationships, employed gainfully, and living in decent housing. And for those returning from prison, those who establish these life patterns are more likely to have successful reentry to their communities. Importantly, a large proportion of men being released from prison hopes to and expects to live with their children. But families and children are negatively affected when parents go into prison, as well as when they return.

Unfortunately, in places characterized by high levels of incarceration, there are additional challenges. Studies of the effects of high incarceration rates in neighborhoods in Oakland have found that important institutions—families and schools, as well as businesses and criminal justice personnel, such as police and parole officers—have become reconfigured to focus on marginalized young boys, increasing the chances that they become more marginalized and involved in crime. Other studies in similar places in Philadelphia have also found that high levels of imprisonment undermined familial, employment, and community relationships, increasing the likelihood of criminal involvement. Additionally, researchers in San Francisco, St. Louis, Seattle, and Washington, D.C., have found that housing, family relationships, marriage, and successful reentry after prison appear to be negatively influenced by high neighborhood levels of incarceration.

More ominously, evidence indicates that these patterns likely have a vicious intergenerational cycle. Children of individuals who have been imprisoned have reduced educational attainment, which obviously bodes ill for their future economic competitiveness. This means that in places with high levels of incarceration, this practice is contributing to another generation that has a heightened likelihood of living in disadvantaged communities. Additionally, researchers have found that judges are more likely to sentence children who come before the juvenile court more harshly if they come from disadvantaged neighborhoods than from more stable communities—yet again continuing the cycle of people moving from disadvantaged places to prison, which makes those neighborhoods more marginalized, which then increases the likelihood of the state removing more people, both juveniles and adults, into the corrections system.

What can be done?

There is an obvious and very straightforward answer to the policy question of how to confront the negative effects of mass incarceration—and that is to reduce it. Mass incarceration did not come about because of substantial increases in crime, but rather because of a set of policy choices that the nation has made. The same simple answer will address the policy question of how to confront the negative impact of mass incarceration on communities of color. Taking this step—reducing mass incarceration—will have profound effects on these communities, because they have disproportionally suffered from the increases in incarceration. And for anyone who may worry, there is no evidence to suggest that a move away from the high level of imprisonment, which characterizes the United States more than any other nation in the world, will result in a substantial increase in crime.

Another important way to address the problems for communities of color is to reduce the residential racial and economic segregation that continues to cause problems for social life in the United States. Admittedly, aiming for this goal will place greater challenges on policymakers and the public alike.

The good news is that there are efforts under way that, if moved forward, would mitigate some of the problems caused by the collateral consequences from imprisonment and some of the negative effects of coercive mobility on communities of color. In 2010, the National Conference of Commissioners on Uniform State Laws proposed the Uniform Collateral Consequences of Criminal Convictions Act, model legislation that might be adopted by the states. If passed, bills such as this would mandate that defendants be advised of all of the collateral consequences that formally accompany felony convictions at the time of sentencing and how they might be mitigated. Currently, courts have no obligation to advise defendants as to these collateral consequences because they are deemed to be "sanctions" rather than punishment. Furthermore, most criminal defense lawyers themselves do not know about or understand the range of collateral consequences that their clients face. In 2013, the National Association of Criminal Defense Lawyers released a book titled *Collateral Consequences of Criminal Convictions: Law, Policy and Practice*, written by Margaret Colgate Love, Jenny Roberts, and Cecelia Klingele and published jointly with Thomson Reuters Westlaw. It is described as "a comprehensive resource for practicing civil and criminal lawyers, judges and policymakers on the legal restrictions and penalties that result from a criminal conviction over and above the court-imposed sentence." Yet, today, most defendants have no idea of the added consequences they will face upon release from incarceration.

It is hoped that discussions around the proposed Uniform Collateral Consequences of Criminal Convictions Act would have the collateral benefit of pressing policymakers to seek out means by which they might mitigate the negative consequences. Since the majority of convictions are the result of plea agreements, defendants might be better informed of the consequences of their decisions. To date, several states, including Vermont, New York, Maryland, and Oregon, as well as the U.S. Virgin Islands, have either enacted or introduced bills that contain elements of the model bill.

States may also elect to opt out of some of the federally mandated collateral consequences for some convictions. For instance, people convicted of drug offenses are, according to federal law, not permitted to receive some "welfare benefits," or to live in federally subsidized housing. This is especially problematic for the families of the convicted, because they are then faced with the choice of receiving these benefits or turning away from the stigmatized family member. The latter option is hard on the maintenance of families and removes from the formerly incarcerated important support systems that enable successful reentry. States are permitted by Congress to opt out of these penalties, but their legislatures need to formally affirmatively enact laws to not have those sanctions applied in their state.

Before federal and state lawmakers decided to get tough on crime by increasing sentencing, most jurisdictions had more robust community services providers for returning prisoners. They were called parole officers. The role of these agents varied from place to place; some of the agents emphasized the police and enforcement aspects of the job, but others emphasized their roles to assist with what is now called reentry. Unfortunately, with the elimination of parole in some states, restrictions on it elsewhere, and declines in budgets for these services, too few people are charged with the responsibility to aid in the reentry process. This is a problem for both the returning individuals and for their families and communities. For example, now that the state of Washington has legalized the recreational use of marijuana, the state is in the process of releasing inmates currently held for possession convictions. One of the young men about to be released told a visiting academic researcher that he was worried because he had no home to return to, no job, and few prospects to help him when he stepped out of the prison door. As far as he knew, the state would not be providing him with reentry assistance. Both the negative effects of imprisonment to individuals and to high-incarceration communities can be mitigated if those returning are aided by having stable housing, their families are supported, and they are assisted in finding and holding employment. Although there were problems with the old sentencing practices and with parole, it was never the case that those systems did not perform important positive functions. Substantial policy changes that create more robust state efforts to support individuals during reentry will not only help them, but their families and, if the coercive mobility thesis is correct, the places they return to as well.

It may be tempting to suggest that those released not be allowed to move back to the communities they lived in when they got into trouble. But the simple truth is that most released prisoners have no place to go other than the communities they know. That is where their families and the people they know are. The likely outcome of such relocation policies would be less successful reentry and greater recidivism. For example, restrictions in some states on where sex offenders can live has led to increased homelessness in this population, making the task of keeping tabs on them more difficult for officials.

Ultimately, the best way to reduce the collateral consequences and the criminogenic effects of high rates of incarceration and their subsequent negative effects for communities of color is to reduce the number of people going into prisons and to create a more just society. On the first front, President Barack Obama recently commuted the sentences of 46 men and women who were serving federal prison time for nonviolent drug offenses, saying: "These men and women were not hardened criminals. But the overwhelming majority had been sentenced to at least 20 years; 14 of them had been sentenced to life for nonviolent drug offenses, so their punishments didn't fit the crime." These and other overly punitive sentences neither serve justice nor protect communities.

It is also clear that continued racial residential segregation exacerbates existing inequalities and fosters severe social and economic disadvantage. More robust enforcement of federal and state fair housing laws will reduce the disparity between minority and majority crime rates. Such action, along with eliminating society's over use of prisons to confront social problems, will substantially reduce the effects of the collateral consequences from incarceration and coercive mobility on communities of color.

> *"If experience indicates that drug activity is concentrated in particular parts of town and that minority groups are overrepresented among people caught with drugs, the police will focus on those groups and parts of town."*

Racial Profiling Is Only Useful in Victimless Crimes

Sheldon Richman

In the following viewpoint, Sheldon Richman argues that law enforcement groups need to use racial profiling for victimless crimes such as selling drugs and firearms because they have no victim to provide descriptions of the perpetrators. The police intentionally target populations whom they know have previously engaged in the criminal behavior. Some people contend that one way to get rid of racial profiling in the war on drugs is to decriminalize the buying and selling of drugs. Sheldon Richman is the former editor of the Freeman *and a contributor to* The Concise Encyclopedia of Economics. *He is the author of* Separating School and State: How to Liberate America's Families *and thousands of articles.*

As you read, consider the following questions:

1. According to the author, when do the police need to use racial profiling for catching criminals and when do they not?
2. What examples does the author use to explain his points about the need for racial profiling?
3. What solution does the author offer to the problem of racial profiling in solving drug crimes?

Virtually everyone wants to be on record opposing racial profiling in law enforcement, the use of race or ethnicity to help determine whom the police should suspect of criminal activity. Nothing is easier than opposing it.

That is understandable. There is something unseemly about targeting someone for a criminal investigation simply because of his skin color or ethnic membership. Those things do not constitute probable cause, and the police shouldn't act like they do.

But beware hypocrisy. One mark of a hypocrisy in politics is the failure to oppose that which necessitates something else one opposes because opposing it would conflict with one's agenda.

For example, few people who decry the role of money in politics go on to oppose what beckons that money: the life-and-death tax and regulatory powers held by government. If you oppose the former, you logically must oppose the latter, which is genesis of the alleged problem. If the government had nothing to sell, no one would be trying to buy. But few are guided by logic on the issue.

Similarly, most people who oppose racial profiling fail to oppose what necessitates it. On the contrary, they enthusiastically support precisely what gives rise to it. Thus protestations against racial profiling are empty posturing designed only to appeal to a set of voters.

Racial profiling is used most often to catch drug sellers and buyers and possessors of guns—in other words, to enforce laws against victimless crimes. It's not needed to catch real criminals—

people who have violated the rights of others by killing, beating, raping, or robbing them. Victims often can describe their assailants to the police. Where no description is available, the police use fingerprinting, DNA, and other evidence-gathering measures. Racial profiling is superfluous.

Take the tragic incident in New York in 1999 when Amadou Diallo, an innocent and unarmed black man, was gunned down by four policemen. Whatever may be said about that tragedy, or its exploitation by Al Sharpton, it was not a case of racial profiling. The police were looking for a man who had raped several black women in Diallo's neighborhood. They had a description of the perpetrator furnished by the victims. Diallo didn't fit a racial profile. He fit the description. Thus the policemen's decision to approach him could hardly have been a case of racial profiling, much less racism. Should they have questioned white males for the sake of fairness?

Racial profiling, on the other hand, is indispensable for catching perpetrators of victimless crimes, such as drug dealing and possession. Why? Because there are no complaining witnesses. The parties to a drug transaction consent and therefore have no reason to describe each other to the police. The authorities would have no way of knowing a drug crime had taken place, much less who committed it. This makes victimless crimes fundamentally different from real crimes. It also makes law enforcement different.

Sting Operations

If all parties to a certain kind of criminal activity do not wish it to come to the attention of the police, the police have a problem. They must find other ways to ferret out evidence of the crime. They will have to rely on wiretaps, searches of residences, street stops of people on the basis of low-level suspicion, and sting operations, such as the one that led to the death of Patrick Dorismond, another innocent man in New York. The police have no other way of catching violators.

But whom shall they target? Obviously, the police will not want to waste time and money with truly random searches and sting operations. Rather, they will focus their efforts for the maximum return. If experience indicates that drug activity is concentrated in particular parts of town and that minority groups are overrepresented among people caught with drugs, the police will focus on those groups and parts of town. That may look like racism, but that's an unlikely explanation. Police win glory by making busts. They have nothing to gain by targeting members of a certain racial group, no matter how much they may dislike that group, if its members rarely engage in the illegal activity. The targeting of groups will tend to have some basis in reality.

Racial profiling is wrong in part because the war on drugs and other victimless activities is wrong. No violation of rights is intrinsic in the buying, selling, or using of drugs. In a free society, consensual activity between adults should not be a crime. If someone violates another's rights while using drugs, the criminal should be punished for the actual crime. Drugs, like alcohol, are no excuse.

We can go further and condemn racial profiling for contravening Western principles of jurisprudence. The Fourth Amendment to the U.S. Constitution states: "The right of the people to be secure in their persons, houses, papers, and effects, against unreasonable searches and seizures, shall not be violated, and no Warrants shall issue, but upon probable cause, supported by Oath or affirmation, and particularly describing the place to be searched, and the persons or things to be seized."

Assume a burglary has occurred in a particular part of town and there is no description of the criminal. However, crime statistics show that young black men are disproportionately represented among convicted burglars. It may indeed be reasonable to guess that the perpetrator is a young black man. But do those facts make the detention and search of all young black men reasonable? Does being young, male, and black in these circumstances constitute probable cause? I don't see how those questions can be answered in the affirmative. And if they are answered affirmatively, what case is there against the state's *preventing* certain people from committing crimes in the first place?

We have been considering what *government* may properly do before or after a crime is committed. Government, as an apparatus of legalized force, is a special case. Private individuals, on the other hand, should be free to act on racial profiles if they wish; specifically, they should be free to avoid certain people and parts of town. Thus taxi and pizza-delivery drivers should not be legally prohibited from exercising their discretion. If these profit maximizers pass up fares and sales to avoid certain areas and customers, they probably have a good reason that has nothing to do with racism.

> *"About that 15 percent of officers who regularly abuse their power: a major problem is they exert an outsize influence on department culture and find support for their actions from ranking officers and police unions."*

Police Culture Supports Institutional Racism

Redditt Hudson

In the following viewpoint, Reddit Hudson argues that many law enforcement agencies employ officers who are racist against the minority populations in which they serve. Police departments are closed communities that protect their own against critics who accuse them of violations of citizens' rights. The media often emphasizes the risk and heroism of police officers instead of holding police departments accountable for violations of citizen rights. Reddit Hudson served in the St. Louis Police Department for five years. He is currently the board chair of The Ethics Project and a member of the National Coalition of Law Enforcement for Justice, Reform, and Accountability.

"I'm a Black Ex-cop, and This is the Real Truth about Race and Policing," Reddit Hudson, Vox Media, May 28, 2015. http://www.vox.com/2015/5/28/8661977/race-police-officer. Reprinted by permission.

As you read, consider the following questions:

1. According to the author, what percent of police officers are racist, nonracist, or could go either way depending on the situation?

2. How do law enforcement agencies support the actions of racist officers?

3. What solutions to the problem of systemic racism in law enforcement agencies does the author suggest?

O n any given day, in any police department in the nation, 15 percent of officers will do the right thing no matter what is happening. Fifteen percent of officers will abuse their authority at every opportunity. The remaining 70 percent could go either way depending on whom they are working with.

That's a theory from my friend K.L. Williams, who has trained thousands of officers around the country in use of force. Based on what I experienced as a black man serving in the St. Louis Police Department for five years, I agree with him. I worked with men and women who became cops for all the right reasons—they really wanted to help make their communities better. And I worked with people like the president of my police academy class, who sent out an email after President Obama won the 2008 election that included the statement, "I can't believe I live in a country full of ni**er lovers!!!!!!!!" He patrolled the streets in St. Louis in a number of black communities with the authority to act under the color of law.

That remaining 70 percent of officers are highly susceptible to the culture in a given department. In the absence of any real effort to challenge department cultures, they become part of the problem. If their command ranks are racist or allow institutional racism to persist, or if a number of officers in their department are racist, they may end up doing terrible things.

It is not only white officers who abuse their authority. The effect of institutional racism is such that no matter what color the officer abusing the citizen is, in the vast majority of those cases of abuse that citizen will be black or brown. That is what is allowed.

And no matter what an officer has done to a black person, that officer can always cover himself in the running narrative of heroism, risk, and sacrifice that is available to a uniformed police officer by virtue of simply reporting for duty. Cleveland police officer Michael Brelo was acquitted of all charges against him in the shooting deaths of Timothy Russell and Malissa Williams, both black and unarmed. Thirteen Cleveland police officers fired 137 shots at them. Brelo, having reloaded at some point during the shooting, fired 49 of the 137 shots. He took his final 15 shots at them after all the other officers stopped firing (122 shots at that point) and, "fearing for his life," he jumped onto the hood of the car and shot 15 times through the windshield.

Not only was this excessive, it was tactically asinine if Brelo believed they were armed and firing. But they weren't armed, and they weren't firing. Judge John O'Donnell acquitted Brelo under the rationale that because he couldn't determine which shots actually killed Russell and Williams, no one is guilty. Let's be clear: this is part of what the Department of Justice means when it describes a "pattern of unconstitutional policing and excessive force."

Nevertheless, many Americans believe that police officers are generally good, noble heroes. A Gallup poll from 2014 asked Americans to rate the honesty and ethical standards of people in various fields: police officers ranked in the top five, just above members of the clergy. The profession—the endeavor—is noble. But this myth about the general goodness of cops obscures the truth of what needs to be done to fix the system. It makes it look like all we need to do is hire good people, rather than fix the entire system. Institutional racism runs throughout our criminal justice system. Its presence in police culture, though often flatly denied by the many police apologists that appear in the media now, has been central to the breakdown in police-community relationships for decades in spite of good people doing police work.

Here's what I wish Americans understood about the men and women who serve in their police departments—and what needs to be done to make the system better for everyone.

1. There are officers who willfully violate the human rights of the people in the communities they serve

As a new officer with the St. Louis in the mid-1990s, I responded to a call for an "officer in need of aid." I was partnered that day with a white female officer. When we got to the scene, it turned out that the officer was fine, and the aid call was canceled. He'd been in a foot pursuit chasing a suspect in an armed robbery and lost him.

The officer I was with asked him if he'd seen where the suspect went. The officer picked a house on the block we were on, and we went to it and knocked on the door. A young man about 18 years old answered the door, partially opening it and peering out at my partner and me. He was standing on crutches. My partner accused him of harboring a suspect. He denied it. He said that this was his family's home and he was home alone.

My partner then forced the door the rest of the way open, grabbed him by his throat, and snatched him out of the house onto the front porch. She took him to the ledge of the porch and, still holding him by the throat, punched him hard in the face and then in the groin. My partner that day snatched an 18-year-old kid off crutches and assaulted him, simply for stating the fact that he was home alone.

I got the officer off of him. But because an aid call had gone out, several other officers had arrived on the scene. One of those officers, who was black, ascended the stairs and asked what was going on. My partner pointed to the young man, still lying on the porch, and said, "That son of a bitch just assaulted me." The black officer then went up to the young man and told him to "get the fuck up, I'm taking you in for assaulting an officer." The young man looked up at the officer and said, "Man ... you see I can't go." His crutches lay not far from him.

The officer picked him up, cuffed him, and slammed him into the house, where he was able to prop himself up by leaning against it. The officer then told him again to get moving to the police car on the street because he was under arrest. The young man told him one last time, in a pleading tone that was somehow angry at the same time, "You see I can't go!" The officer reached down and grabbed both the young man's ankles and yanked up. This caused the young man to strike his head on the porch. The officer then dragged him to the police car. We then searched the house. No one was in it.

These kinds of scenes play themselves out everyday all over our country in black and brown communities. Beyond the many unarmed blacks killed by police, including recently Freddie Gray in Baltimore, other police abuses that don't result in death foment resentment, distrust, and malice toward police in black and brown communities all over the country. Long before Darren Wilson shot and killed unarmed Michael Brown last August, there was a poisonous relationship between the Ferguson, Missouri, department and the community it claimed to serve. For example, in 2009 Henry Davis was stopped unlawfully in Ferguson, taken to the police station, and brutally beaten while in handcuffs. He was then charged for bleeding on the officers' uniforms after they beat him.

2. The bad officers corrupt the departments they work for

About that 15 percent of officers who regularly abuse their power: a major problem is they exert an outsize influence on department culture and find support for their actions from ranking officers and police unions. Chicago is a prime example of this: the city has created a reparations fund for the hundreds of victims who were tortured by former Chicago Police Commander Jon Burge and officers under his command from the 1970s to the early '90s.

The victims were electrically shocked, suffocated, and beaten into false confessions that resulted in many of them being convicted and serving time for crimes they didn't commit. One man, Darrell Cannon, spent 24 years in prison for a crime he confessed to but didn't commit. He confessed when officers repeatedly appeared to load a shotgun and after doing so each time put it in his mouth and pulled the trigger. Other men received electric shocks until they confessed.

The torture was systematic, and the culture that allowed for it is systemic. I call your attention to the words "and officers under his command." Police departments are generally a functioning closed community where people know who is doing what. How many officers "under the command" of Commander Burge do you think didn't know what was being done to these men? How many do you think were uncomfortable with the knowledge? Ultimately, though, they were okay with it. And Burge got four years in prison, and now receives his full taxpayer-funded pension.

3. The mainstream media helps sustain the narrative of heroism that even corrupt officers take refuge in

This is critical to understanding why police-community relations in black and brown communities across the country are as bad as they are. In [an] interview with Fox News, former New York City Police Commissioner Howard Safir never acknowledges the lived experience of thousands and thousands of blacks in New York, Baltimore, Ferguson, or anywhere in the country. In fact, he seems to be completely unaware of it. This allows him to leave viewers with the impression that the recent protests against police brutality are baseless, and that allegations of racism are "totally wrong—just not true." The reality of police abuse is not limited to a number of "very small incidents" that have impacted black people nationwide, but generations of experienced and witnessed abuse.

The media is complicit in this myth-making: the interviewer does not ever challenge Howard Safir. She doesn't point out, for example, the over $1 billion in settlements the NYPD has paid out over the last decade and a half for the misconduct of its officers. She doesn't reference the numerous accounts of actual black or Hispanic

NYPD officers who have been profiled and even assaulted without cause when they were out of uniform by white NYPD officers.

No matter what an officer has done to a black person, that officer can always cover himself in the running narrative of heroism

Instead she leads him with her questions to reference the heroism, selflessness, risk, and sacrifice that are a part of the endeavor that is law enforcement, but very clearly not always characteristic of police work in black and brown communities. The staging for this interview—US flag waving, somber-faced officers—is wash, rinse, and repeat with our national media.

When you take a job as a police officer, you do so voluntarily. You understand the risks associated with the work. But because you signed on to do a dangerous job does not mean you are then allowed to violate the human rights, civil rights, and civil liberties of the people you serve. It's the opposite. You should protect those rights, and when you don't you should be held accountable. That simple statement will be received by police apologists as "anti-cop." It is not.

4. Cameras provide the most objective record of police-citizen encounters available

When Walter Scott was killed by officer Michael Slager in South Carolina last year, the initial police report put Scott in the wrong. It stated that Scott had gone for Slager's Taser, and Slager was in fear for his life. If not for the video recording that later surfaced, the report would have likely been taken by many at face value. Instead we see that Slager shot Scott repeatedly and planted the Taser next to his body after the fact.

Every officer in the country should be wearing a body camera that remains activated throughout any interaction they have with the public while on duty. There is no reasonable expectation of privacy for officers when they are on duty and in service to the public. Citizens must also have the right to record police officers as they carry out their public service, provided that they are at a safe distance, based on the circumstances, and not interfering. Witnessing an interaction does not by itself constitute interference.

5. There are officers around the country who want to address institutional racism

The National Coalition of Law Enforcement Officers for Justice, Reform and Accountability is a new coalition of current and former law enforcement officers from around the nation. Its mission is to fight institutional racism in our criminal justice system and police culture, and to push for accountability for police officers that abuse their power.

Many of its members are already well-established advocates for criminal justice reform in their communities. It's people like former Sergeant De Lacy Davis of New Jersey, who has worked to change police culture for years. It's people like former LAPD Captain John Mutz, who is white, and who is committed to working to build a system where everyone is equally valued. His colleagues from the LAPD —former Sergeant Cheryl Dorsey, now a frequent CNN contributor (providing some much-needed perspective), and former officer Alex Salazar, who worked LAPD's Rampart unit— are a part of this effort. Several NYPD officers, many of whom are founding members of 100 Blacks in Law Enforcement Who Care, the gold standard for black municipal police organizations, are a part of this group. Vernon Wells, Noel Leader, Julian Harper, and Cliff Hollingsworth, to name a few, are serious men with a serious record of standing up for their communities against police abuse. There's also Rochelle Bilal, a former sergeant out of Philadelphia, Sam Costales out of New Mexico, former Federal Marshal Matthew Fogg, and many others.

These men and women are ready to reach out to the thousands of officers around the country who have been looking for a national law enforcement organization that works to remake police culture. The first priority is accountability—punishment—for officers who willfully abuse the rights and bodies of those they are sworn to serve. Training means absolutely nothing if officers don't adhere to it and are not held accountable when they don't. It is key to any meaningful reform.

Police abuse in black and brown communities is generations old. It is nothing new.

Racism is woven into the fabric of our nation. At no time in our history has there been a national consensus that everyone should be equally valued in all areas of life. We are rooted in racism in spite of the better efforts of Americans of all races to change that.

Because of this legacy of racism, police abuse in black and brown communities is generations old. It is nothing new. It has become more visible to mainstream America largely because of the proliferation of personal recording devices, cellphone cameras, video recorders—they're everywhere. We need police officers. We also need them to be held accountable to the communities they serve.

> *"Cops are a special breed, selected to be willing and able to withstand adversity because of our deep love for humanity."*

Police Are Committed to Protecting All Lives

Tim Barfield

In the following viewpoint, Tim Barfield argues that police serve and protect black communities. Some police officers contend that accusations of racism toward them are misplaced. Every day, they say, they are protecting black communities where they are often met with threats of violence and uncooperative victims. Black lives seem to matter more to the police protecting them than to the perpetrators who are committing the crimes. Tim Barfield has served as a police officer for thirty-five years.

As you read, consider the following questions:

1. According to the author, what has driven both white and black families out of inner cities to safer suburbs?
2. What does the author think motivates police officers to put their lives at risk each day?
3. How does the author think the Black Lives Matter movement obstructs police from creating safer communities?

"Black Lives Matter to the Thin Blue Line," Tim Barfield, Law Officer, July 24, 2016. www.lawofficer.com. Reprinted by permission.

The narrative being portrayed by the liberal media, BLM and the man that holds the Office of the President is that police are shooting black Americans because they consider them no more important than dogs. How else does the message make any sense? Their portrayal that black Americans are shot by police without provocation or that a police officer should be willing to die rather than defend themselves is not even logical. The recurring theme is that police officers do not care about black Americans. I would argue that they care more about black lives than most in the BLM movement.

I spent many years in a community that began changing thirty years ago. During that time, when people moved from an area that was changing, it was called "white flight". Even then some were trying to portray the issue as black and white. As someone who lived in the community and also dealt with the problems on the front line every day, I was troubled by people who WANT to see everything by color. Martin Luther King, Jr. wanted people to be judged by their character and for color to be inconsequential. The forms we fill out, the surveys we take and the statistics we see every day keep directing us back toward our differences and not our common concerns.

It was not the color that drove people out of that community, it was the values that people had. My family lived across the street from some white "trash". The kids were disrespectful, loud, rude and generally unlikeable. Also, one house over was a "black" family. I remember a conversation with that "black" neighbor about the obnoxious neighbor that he shared a property line with. He was troubled because he moved out of the bigger city to the suburbs to get away from people who did not share his values, like the "white" trash. We were great neighbors, all of us with the exception of the people who did not share our values. We thought that respect for other's property, looking out for one another, keeping property values up and kind words spoken in the neighborhood were the important things from neighbors. We liked people who taught their children respect, to stay out of trouble and keeping the

DATA SHOWS DISPROPORTIONATE ARREST AND CONVICTION RATES

The recent protests and conversations over #blacklivesmatter show the United States is in no way post-racial. The debate rages on as both sides ask, "Is America's criminal justice system colorblind?" The best way to know is to look at the data.

[...]

The national arrest rates for marijuana possession were 716 arrests per 100,000 black residents in 2010 and 192 arrests per 100,000 white residents. Marijuana arrests accounted for over half of all drug arrests in 2010, according to the ACLU.

[...]

The majority of people serving life sentences at the federal level are black, and almost half of those serving life sentences nationally are black. In some states, the percentage is even higher: In Maryland, 77.4 percent of inmates serving life sentences are black, in Georgia it's 72 percent and for Mississippi, 71.5 percent, according to research from The Sentencing Project. The ACLU also found authorization to seek the death penalty was more likely when there was at least one white victim in the case. Between December 2007 and September 2011, the sentences for black male offenders are almost 20 percent longer than sentences for white male offenders, according to data from the U.S. Sentencing Commission.

"No, Justice is Not Colorblind," Lindsey Cook, *U.S. News*, December 11, 2014.

neighborhood a place of peace and safety. As the neighborhood changed, it was the values of the people who moved in that was a problem, not the color. I have worked with, lived with and been friends with all kinds of people. Rude, loud, disrespectful people who don't care about what people think about them, who don't care about their neighbors, their neighbors stuff or the neighborhood itself aren't the kind of people anybody wants to live by. In fact, in most instances, it should have not been called "white flight" but "black flight" because in most cases the "black" Americans who moved out, moved out to get away from the values of the people they left behind.

One call that had a profound impact on me many years ago went like this. I remember going to a fight call between two black youths at the end of the street I lived on. While talking to witnesses, I found an older black man leaning on his rake. When I asked him what happened his statement was, "You know officer, I left B.H. (a nearby city he moved from) to get away from nig…s like this." He explained that he thought moving to our city would allow him to be around people who shared his values.

I would often get complaints of racism from negligent parents or thugs who looked for an excuse to exonerate the arrested person. The facts did not support either their release or the racism charge. BLM wants to make a stand on people who are committing crimes or refuse to comply. Who are they helping?

If the police wanted to "kill" blacks all they would have to do is get out of the way.

The truth is that police officers of all different backgrounds run toward the violence and risk their lives every day to save the very people they are being told they hate. During violent crime investigations, officers are often met with an uncooperative victim who would rather protect a thug than help the police. What would possess a person to risk their lives to help people who don't want help or run into violence to protect people they "hate".

Police officers are humans. We see things that can never be removed from our memory yet move forward to help. Even today, when the ranks can't be filled because of the portrayal of police to the public, the thin blue line goes to work and responds to the calls. To be accused of this type of hatred after what we do and see would make a lesser person crumble but not a police officer. They keep coming back.

All lives matter to the thin blue line and that is why we do what we do. It is not the bullying, the great pay or the violence and hate directed toward us. Cops are a special breed, selected to be willing and able to withstand adversity because of our deep love for humanity.

Let's join ranks and become color blind by working on values that we all share. We should love our kids, our neighbors and our neighborhoods. There was a time in this country where we all shared in the values of Mark 12:30-31, "Love the Lord your God with all your heart and with all your soul and with all your mind and with all your strength. The second is this: Love your neighbor as yourself. There is no commandment greater than these."

Periodical and Internet Sources Bibliography

The following articles have been selected to supplement the diverse views presented in this chapter.

Matt Ferner, "New Report Details Devastating Effects of Mass Incarceration on the U.S.," *Huffington Post*, May 2, 2016.

Brad Heath, "Racial Gap in U.S. Arrest Rates: 'Staggering Disparity,'" *USA Today*, November 19, 2014.

Steven Hsieh, "14 Disturbing Stats About Racial Inequality in American Public Schools," *Nation*, March 21, 2014.

Andrew Kahn and Chris Kirk, "What It's Like to be Black in the Criminal Justice System," *Slate.com,* August 9, 2015.

Sharon LaFraniere and Andrew W. Lehren, "The Disproportionate Risks of Driving While Black," *New York Times*, October 24, 2015.

Heather MacDonald, "Police Shootings and Race," *Washington Post*, July 18, 2016.

Kia Makarechi, "What the Data Really Says About Police and Racial Bias," *Vanity Fair*, July 14, 2016.

National Association for the Advancement of Colored People, "Criminal Justice Fact Sheet," NAACP.org, 2016.

Edwin S. Rubenstein, "The Color of Crime, 2016 Revised Edition," *American Renaissance,* 2016.

Emily Von Hoffmann, "How Incarceration Infects a Community," *Atlantic,* March 6, 2015.

Alia Won, "How School Suspensions Push Black Students Behind," *Atlantic,* February 8, 2016.

OPPOSING
VIEWPOINTS®
SERIES

CHAPTER 4

Can the United States Overcome its History of Racism?

Chapter Preface

On July 13, 2016, US Senator Tim Scott, of South Carolina, gave a speech to Congress in response to the violent confrontations between black citizens and police officers in Texas, Minnesota, and Louisiana that had rocked the nation that summer. In it, he described the numerous times as a black man he had been stopped while driving by members of law enforcement for what he called trivial reasons. He recalled being stopped seven times in one year. Then he spoke about one incident that exemplified the experiences of many African Americans in the United States:

> So it's easy to identify a U.S. Senator by our pin. I recall walking into an office building just last year after being here for five years on the Capitol, and the officer looked at me, a little attitude and said, "The pin, I know. You, I don't. Show me your ID." I'll tell you, I was thinking to myself, either he thinks I'm committing a crime—impersonating a member of Congress—or, or what? Well, I'll tell you that later that evening I received a phone call from his supervisor apologizing for the behavior. Mr. President, that is at least the third phone call that I've received from a supervisor or the chief of police since I've been in the Senate.

Statistics show that minorities in the United States are often victims of racial disparities in traffic stops, which can sometimes end in tragedies, such as with Philando Castile in Minnesota and Sandra Bland in Texas. Many communities are working toward ending what has been perceived as discriminatory policing, in which people of color are challenged in numbers disproportionate to their presence in the community.

Data also shows disparities in other areas, such as college admission, homeownership rates, and income. Many public policies left over from pre-civil rights eras have persisted, locking out people of color from neighborhoods with affordable housing and safe schools. Without adequate education and access to jobs and training, minorities do not earn the income that allows them to buy homes, accrue wealth, and achieve economic security.

Efforts to rectify this lack of access have sometimes included affirmative action policies that have also been called discriminatory. One case, *Fisher v. University of Texas*, made it to the Supreme Court, which in 2016 ruled that universities may continue to consider race as a factor in ensuring a diverse student body. However, the defendant in the case, Texas student Abigail Fisher, warned of the unintended consequences of race-based admissions. Those minorities whose achievements are due to their own merits risk being accused of using affirmative action to secure their spots.

In September 2016, President Obama addressed the nation in one of his final speeches to the country regarding race in America. The occasion was the opening of the National Museum of African American History and Culture in Washington, DC. During his speech, he spoke of the issues that divide white and minority Americans:

> A museum alone will not alleviate poverty in every inner city, or every rural hamlet. It won't eliminate gun violence from all our neighborhoods, or immediately ensure that justice is always color-blind. It won't wipe away every instance of discrimination in a job interview, or a sentencing hearing, or folks trying to rent an apartment.

However, he made his opinion clear on the issue of overcoming racism:

> And so hopefully this museum can help us talk to each other. And more importantly, listen to each other. And most importantly, see each other—Black and White and Latino and Native American, and Asian American—see how our stories are bound together.

> "The solution to racial inequality must
> be an economic one, in addition to
> being a social one, a political one,
> a judicial one, and, above all, a
> human one."

Racial Problems are American Problems

Matt Bernhard

In the following viewpoint, Matt Berhnard argues that solving the problems of racial injustice in the United States is not just an enormous task for the racial minorities who suffer from the results of the injustices. They did not create the racist systems that impoverished populations of people of color. Our country can come together when everyone takes responsibility to eliminate the systematic racism that underlies our educational, criminal justice, economic, and political institutions. Matt Bernhard is a graduate student and blogger.

As you read, consider the following questions:

1. Why does the author think that minority populations are unable to overcome systemic racial injustice?
2. Why does the author think all Americans have a responsibility to work toward equality for minorities?
3. According to the author, how has American history contributed to systemic racism?

I recently came across some comments made by Stephen A. Smith in reaction to controversial comments made by Martin O'Malley about the #BlackLivesMatter movement. While I deeply respect what Smith is doing in attempting to keep the dialog about racial wounds in the US alive, I find his reasoning problematic. He posits that it is incumbent on black people to overcome the systematic disadvantages that have been dealt to them. To defend this, Stephen A. invoked black-on-black crime as a justification for his claims of hypocrisy in the #BlackLivesMatter movement. While his point is not without merit, I would argue that the reason for incredibly high rates of black-on-black crime comes first and foremost from the immensity of the tragedy of low socioeconomic status in the black community. Attempting to devalue the #BlackLivesMatter movement because "black folks are killing black folks" entirely misses this point, and puts up an impossible barrier by saying the only way to get out is to accept the injustice. Not that I wish to discourage a self-reliant ethos or rugged individualism, merely that I find this reasoning dangerously close to that used by racists to talk about the racial divide. You know the type, the older, middle class white man who says things like, and pardon the language, "I just don't understand why these n*****s can't stop acting like n*****s."

The problem first and foremost with putting the majority of the burden of overcoming the social, economic, educational, judicial, legal, geographic, and otherwise (hereafter referred to as systemic) disadvantages on the black community alone is that it asks the impossible. If it weren't impossible, why haven't black people overcome systemic injustice yet? The issue of race in the United States is far too complicated and intertwined to think that it can depend on the actions of only one subcommunity. For every black person that has ever had the ability, the will, and the luck to overcome the system, there have been 10 more who have not been so fortunate, and 100 more rules, regulations, and people standing in their way. Furthermore, if we consider, hypothetically, what happens if an entire subdivision of society were to overcome such tremendous systemic disadvantages alone, we can see that the result is not pleasant. Black folks would be incredibly bitter that not only did they have to overcome immense socioeconomic challenges in the throwing off of the chains of oppression, but also that they had to do it alone. On the other hand, the white community would be equally bitter, and not just the racist segments. Seeing an entire group of people get ahead long enough to catch up to the median of society would undoubtedly make whites believe they had been cheated in some way. Granted, I am making **incredible** overgeneralizations here, and this is wild speculation. I don't want to dwell in this place any longer, so I am going to move on.

The problem that I just ran into, and the problem that we run into every time we try to frame the racial chasm in this country in terms of black and white, is that it isn't a problem that can be simply reduced to its constituent parts. For one, this oversimplification entirely ignores other people who face the exact same systemic oppression: Latinos, who fare about as well as blacks in American society, Native Americans, who on average fare even worse than blacks, Asian and white people who are struggling in society for reasons not entirely dissimilar than those faced by blacks, women, those who are discriminated against for their sexual preference, etc. Not to mention the fact that each of those groups is infinitely divisible within themselves and across boundaries into a myriad of origins, ethnicities, religions, so on and so forth. This is what Martin O'Malley (I hope) was trying to get at: that attempting to assign colors to find a solution to this problem simply doesn't work. We just get stuck back where we started. We shouldn't try to fix problems that arose because of color classification with color classification. The only colors that should apply as far as a solution to systemic racial injustice is concerned are red, white, and blue. This is not a black problem, or a white problem, or any other kind of problem; this is an American problem.

This is not to say that we can pretend that races don't exist; that would be simply ignoring the roots and expression of the problem. We also run the risk of signaling to people that race doesn't matter, and moreover **their** race doesn't matter. The manner in which racial wounds are healed is not by ignoring that they are, in fact, racial. When we attempt to move from "Black Lives Matter" to "All Lives Matter", there is an implicit assumption that being black cannot be a positive thing, and we have to cover over it by applying more general terms. In effect, we signal that being black is of less value than being anything else. Approaching the problem with an all-encompassing solution would be ideal, but a solution that attempts to paint over the wide range of differences between and among racial communities is not a solution.

This is what I mean when I say that racial problems in America are American problems. The immense diversity that has allowed the United States to thrive all throughout its history must be part of the dialog as we work toward closing the gaps. We cannot ignore the fact that a non-trivial component of this greatness was built through an overtly racist system that unfairly leveraged that diversity. Any time we can systematically oppress or otherwise disadvantage an entire group of people for an arbitrary reason such as race, we can create cheap labor with which to produce a greater number and variety of goods. If we wish to amend racial inequality, the solution must take this into consideration as well. My hope is that some day a society may exist in which no group of people has to be oppressed, for whatever reason, so that the rest may have every freedom, opportunity, and security that status as a human being confers. The solution to racial inequality must be an economic one, in addition to being a social one, a political one, a judicial one, and, above all, a human one.

My point here is not to say, "Behold! A cure-all to race problems in the United States." Anyone who attempts to pitch a solution like that is selling snake oil, and you should run away as fast as you can. Moreover, I haven't actually proposed any sort of solution, I've merely attempted to paint in broad strokes how a blurry picture of the solution may some day look. My point is mostly to reframe the problem, so that we can have a more intelligent and productive discussion about fixing it. It is an American problem, that can only be solved by Americans. If we do not solve it and alleviate

Minorities Are Often Subjected to Microaggressions

[Derald Wing] Sue first proposed a classification of racial microaggressions in a 2007 article on how they manifest in clinical practice in the *American Psychologist* (Vol. 2, No. 4). There, he notes three types of current racial transgressions:

Microassaults: Conscious and intentional actions or slurs, such as using racial epithets, displaying swastikas or deliberately serving a white person before a person of color in a restaurant.

Microinsults: Verbal and nonverbal communications that subtly convey rudeness and insensitivity and demean a person's racial heritage or identity. An example is an employee who asks a colleague of color how she got her job, implying she may have landed it through an affirmative action or quota system.

Microinvalidations: Communications that subtly exclude, negate or nullify the thoughts, feelings or experiential reality of a person of color. For instance, white people often ask Asian-Americans where they were born, conveying the message that they are perpetual foreigners in their own land.

Sue focuses on microinsults and microinvalidations because of their less obvious nature, which puts people of color in a psychological bind, he asserts: While the person may feel insulted, she is not sure exactly why, and the perpetrator doesn't acknowledge that anything has happened because he is not aware he has been offensive.

"Unmasking 'racial micro aggressions," Tori DeAngelis, *Monitor on Psychology*, 2009, Vol 40, No. 2.

the suffering in the black community (and every other community that suffers at the hands of systemic injustice), Americans are the ones getting hurt. The question shouldn't be, how much longer are we willing to let black people suffer, the question should be how much longer are we willing to let ourselves, the American people, suffer?

> "When people of color challenge racism, we aren't just challenging what whites do, we're challenging an aspect of who they are, and from the position of the inferiors in a racial hierarchy that is held together in no small part by white entitlement."

Eliminating Racism Requires Personal Transformation

Scot Nakagawa

In the following viewpoint, Scot Nakagawa argues that the United States was founded upon racist ideas. For settlers it was a land of opportunity, but only for European immigrants. White Americans need to realize that they have a core of racist beliefs, which is why racism persists despite changing political, economic, and demographic conditions. Though this realization doesn't negate the need for improvements in these conditions, real change won't happen until Americans address the negative stereotypes and acknowledge the prejudices inside them. Scot Nakagawa serves as senior partner at ChangeLab, a racial justice laboratory.

"For Racial Healing, We Need To Get Real about Racism," Scot Nakagawa, Transformation, July 2, 2013. Reprinted by permission.

As you read, consider the following questions:

1. How does the author use his own experiences as an Asian American to explain his theories about racism?
2. Why does the author believe that racism arises from internal beliefs rather than external experiences?
3. In what ways does the author think that whites and racial minorities can resolve the issues of racism in the United States?

Here's a provocative statement. The reason white Americans are so touchy about racism is precisely because white supremacy is ingrained in white identity. When people of color challenge racism, we aren't just challenging what whites do, we're challenging an aspect of who they are, and from the position of the inferiors in a racial hierarchy that is held together in no small part by white entitlement.

In order to reconcile ourselves to one another, we need to get real about the forces that fragment us, especially race. But overcoming racial divisions will require us to go beyond politics as usual and invest ourselves in personal transformation.

Why? We live in a society that has so deeply internalized race, that race, and by extension racism, is at the very core of who we are as a people. As Americans, our history of racism is the story of us. Until we deal with that, we will never coalesce across the divisions that history has created.

But if white people were the only problem, racism would be resolved by demographic change. Yet demographic change will not end racism.

Race was, for most of U.S. history, an important system of political and social organization. The rationale for imposing that system wasn't just internalized by whites. We have *all* internalized race, though with strikingly different consequences.

The notion of "white devils" running around among us only strengthens racism. Simplistic ideas of good and evil are integral to the racial categories upon which racism is founded. Deciding that certain people are morally deficient because of race only strengthens those categories.

Instead of relying on simple good vs evil dichotomies of race, I often picture America as a broken mirror. Each fragment reflects some aspect of who we are as a people. But the images they reflect are so incomplete that trying to make sense of them is next to impossible.

Even many of the dominant themes of American culture are essentially racist tropes.

Take for instance the American Dream. It's founded in the belief that America is a land of freedom in which hard work will yield opportunity. But America is a nation founded in slavery. The slave trade capitalized the original colonies and eventually the project of creating the United States of America.

Because of slavery, the U.S. was founded as a land of opportunity, but only for European immigrants. This reality persisted all the way up to the end of the Civil War, a conflict that ended less than 150 years ago. That's real.

White immigrants were drawn to America in order to escape the rigid European class system and achieve the dream of becoming gentry in the New World. The economy they entered relied on a racial caste system that favored whites. White people's dream of social mobility had nothing to do with black slaves and would continue to have very little to do with their descendants, even through the mid-twentieth century rise of the American middle class.

With slavery as its economic engine, the U.S. expanded across the continent. Americans won territory by engaging in genocidal campaigns against the original people of North America.

In spite of this history, we call ourselves a "nation of immigrants." The very notion is rooted in our history of excluding African Americans and Native people from citizenship, making the U.S. historically, indeed, a nation made up only of immigrants. That's also real. Yet we conflate the idea of the "nation of immigrants" with liberty and justice for all.

We continue to organize our understanding of America according to race today. Consider the Asian American "model minority" stereotype. The stereotype is rooted in the 1960s when it was deployed to undercut support for the Civil Rights Movement.

Asians in America like me were described during this period as compliant, uncomplaining strivers, as compared with black people, who were cast as a "problem minority." Asians were said to have channeled our concerns about racial injustice into hard work, winning success and supposedly putting the lie to the claim on the part of black leaders that government action was required to resolve persistent black poverty.

The reality is that Asian American "success" is by no means cultural. It is a political construct.

Asian America is a hodge podge of ethnic groups, many of which have benefited from the gains of the Civil Rights Movement. Many others were recruited to the U.S. to fulfill our need for certain classes of highly skilled workers. Because of special visas, those with higher educations and higher incomes are over-represented among Asian Americans.

Yet Asian Americans actually make less per capita than whites. Asian household incomes skew higher, both because we tend to be concentrated in expensive coastal cities where wages are inflated, and because we have more incomes per household on average.

But race is so powerful a force in shaping our understanding of one another that the "model minority" stereotype has become accepted as fact. Some have even gone so far as to suggest that genetics play a factor in Asian American achievement.

As a racial justice advocate and community organizer, I've had to learn to live with this reality. In the 1970s, the angry young man I was believed that race is a political system requiring political solutions. We would win racial equity only by appealing to political and economic self-interest. Anything else was just feel-good politics; they might feel nice but they're ultimately a waste of time.

But over the years my cynicism eroded, replaced by the recognition that in spite of all of the organizing I was doing, work magnified many times over by the efforts of thousands of campaigns for racial justice waged by people far cleverer than me, racism adapts to changing circumstances and persists in ever more insidious forms.

Racism is not just a political problem. It lives in our hearts and we live it every day through our shared culture. All of us do, even if we may experience race differently, and many of us to our disadvantage.

We are, indeed, a broken mirror. *To truly understand human need and find our way to a just peace, we must commit to the slow and painstaking work of pulling the jagged shards of that mirror together so that with each touch we become a truer reflection of what it means to be human.*

This will require honest dialogue, and a willingness to invest as much in cross-racial community building as we do in campaigns and public policy. Through expanding our relationship networks we expand our perspectives, ideally in ways that redefine our sense of community need.

We need to conduct a people's archeology of race. If the story of race is the story of us, what are the many threads of this story and how do they inform our sense of who we are?

I've witnessed this kind of work many times. I've stood in circles with the families of incarcerated people, naming our fears, claiming our weaknesses, and helping each other find the strength to continue to struggle to change Departments of Corrections and public opinion concerning our loved ones. The process doesn't just involve "feel-goodisms". It also requires us to name the negative stereotypes we've developed concerning one another so that when they are used against us we aren't divided by unacknowledged prejudices lurking beneath the surface.

In multi-ethnic groups of Asian Americans and Pacific Islanders, we've shared the stories of how our families came to be in the U.S., or how the U.S. came to claim our families and homelands.

And as we tell our stories, we do as much to acknowledge privilege as to describe our oppression. The stories are charted. Timelines and maps are often created. We acknowledge that the oppression of Asian America is not just the story of racist immigration quotas, hate crimes, and exploitation. It is also our story, and the extent to which we've accepted certain privileges of being American, or even of being stereotyped as model Americans.

In this way, we can nourish the kind of genuine solidarity needed to win real change.

> *"By striking down Section 4 of the VRA and ignoring the clear words of the Fifteenth Amendment, Roberts is elevating white America's racial fatigue into constitutional law."*

Perceived Equalities Can Mean a Step Backward For Minorities

Jamelle Bouie

In the following viewpoint, Jamelle Bouie argues that governmental bodies exhibit fatigue in the country's fight for equal rights. When the Supreme Court overturned Section 4 of the 1965 Voting Rights Act, some former Confederate states were able to pass voter identification laws that could potentially disenfranchise hundreds of thousands of people. The right to vote for former slaves and their ancestors has been a hard-fought battle and is still not completely achieved. The Supreme Court ruling represents the fatigue of the country in the struggle to overcome its racist past. Jamelle Bouie is a staff writer at the American Prospect.

"America's Fatigue in the Fight Against Racism," Jamelle Bouie, *American Prospect*, June 25, 2013. www.prospect.org. Reprinted by permission.

As you read, consider the following questions:

1. According to the author, what is the purpose of Section 4 of the 1965 Voting Rights Act?
2. What rationale did Chief Justice John Roberts give in his ruling to overturn the law?
3. Why does the author think that Section 4 is still needed?

The stated purpose of the Civil War Amendments was to arm Congress with the power and authority to protect all persons within the Nation from violations of their rights by the States," writes Justice Ruth Bader Ginsburg in her dissent against the five justices who ruled to overturn Section 4 of the Voting Rights Act (VRA) today.

The reason for citing this fact of history is straightforward: In it resides the core dispute of *Shelby County, Alabama v. Holder*, the case decided by the Supreme Court this morning.

The Fifteenth Amendment to the Constitution was the last of the three Civil War amendments and arguably the most controversial. It was one thing to emancipate the slaves (the Thirteenth Amendment) or guarantee equal protection under the law (the Fourteenth Amendment), but the Fifteenth granted suffrage to black men, which was a bridge too far for many whites, in both the North and South. To Southern politicians of the time, it was "the most revolutionary measure" to ever pass Congress.

The full text of the amendment is as such: "The right of citizens of the United States to vote shall not be denied or abridged by the United States or by any State on account of race, color, or previous condition of servitude." What's more, "The Congress shall have power to enforce this article by appropriate legislation."

For nearly a century after its passage, the first clause was all but unenforced. States—in the South and otherwise—were permitted to restrict the franchise for blacks through use of poll taxes, literacy tests, grandfather clauses, and broad criminal codes that required disenfranchisement for the smallest offenses. The Voting Rights

Act, as Justice Ginsburg explains, was Congress' attempt to actualize the second clause of the Fifteenth Amendment, and begin to fix the abuses of the past.

In particular, Section 4 of the law sets down a formula to identify which state and local governments with a history of racial discrimination are required to "pre-clear" (a provision of Section 5) changes to voting law with the federal government. By and large, these are the states of the former Confederacy and other areas with a history of low black turnout and laws that sought to reduce black voting.

In his opinion—speaking for the 5–4 majority—Chief Justice John Roberts takes pains to emphasize the extent to which he isn't opposed to the goal of ending racial discrimination in voting. He just doesn't believe the current formula reflects the progress of the last 40 years, particularly in terms of black turnout and rates of officeholding. Striking it down gives Congress a chance to reevaluate the formula, and to devise one that reflects the conditions of the present moment.

This sounds reasonable, but there are two facts that make this an extraordinary decision. First, it ignores the extent to which Congress built flexibility into the VRA with its 2006 reauthorization, which passed with near-unanimous support after months of investigation and intensive hearings. For instance, if a state or local government can show a decade of compliance—as well as progress toward remedying racial discrimination in voting—it can receive an exemption. The states and localities that continue to fall under pre-clearance are those that show ongoing patterns of discrimination *on top* of meeting the standards set out in Section 4. "All told," notes Ginsburg, "between 1982 and 2006, DOJ objections blocked over 700 voting changes based on a determination that the changes were discriminatory." In reauthorizing the VRA with the same formula, Congress emphasized the extent to which it felt comfortable with this continued vigilance. To cite progress as a reason for striking it down, Ginsburg writes, "is like throwing away your umbrella in a rainstorm because you are not getting wet."

The second thing relates back to the Fifteenth Amendment. Yes, Roberts says that Congress can revisit Section 4 and devise a new formula. But the reality is this: There's little chance that Republicans in either chamber would sign on to revising the VRA. Which means that, for all intents and purposes, pre-clearance—which relies on Section 4 for its teeth—is no longer in effect. If Congress was trying to fulfill the mandate of the Fifteenth by reauthorizing the VRA, then Roberts has said, "No, you can't, because times have *changed*."

The problem is that our long history of apartheid, discrimination, and white supremacy requires an equally long attempt at repair and reconciliation. It's why the 2006 reauthorization extended the VRA for another quarter century: because "40 years has not been a sufficient amount of time to eliminate the vestiges of discrimination following nearly 100 years of disregard for the dictates of the 15th amendment," the law's authors note.

The last three years are proof positive of this assessment. Writing for *Colorlines*, Brentin Mock notes that four states—Virginia, North Carolina, Alabama, and Mississippi—have passed voter identification laws that could disenfranchise hundreds of thousands of people, the large majority of whom are African Americans. The Justice Department was able to block these under pre-clearance, but the Court's ruling now means they can go forward. It's also not hard to find information on Republican-passed laws that restricted early voting, made registration more difficult, closed polling locations (almost always in predominantly minority precincts), and created new, more onerous requirements for casting a ballot. These laws are largely the reason that African Americans waited in line to vote nearly twice as long as their white counterparts. That this occurred mostly in the states of the former Confederacy (the ones formerly covered by pre-clearance) is no accident.

A whole host of people—with far more expertise than I'll ever have—will debate this ruling for a long time. But at the risk of hyperbole, I think it's worth offering a few early thoughts on what it might mean in the broad history of this country's fight for racial equality.

It is difficult to overstate the extent to which racism is tied to the history of this country. Without slavery, the Declaration of Independence is hard to imagine. Without fealty to Jim Crow, there is no New Deal. At various points however—the Civil War, Reconstruction, and the Civil Rights Movement—we have tried to loosen our bonds to racism and rectify the evil of the past. Each time, we make genuine progress. The 1890s were a time of savage violence and disadvantage for African Americans, but they weren't enslaved. Blacks were still far behind the mainstream in the 1970s, but they had gained new opportunities for advancement. But to fully disentangle racism from national life requires a tremendous amount of energy. After all, you don't just need to provide formal equality or encourage tolerance, you need to reform the whole system—the full range of institutions that privilege whites at the expense of blacks and other minorities.

Americans have never been able to commit to that project. Reconstruction was a start, and it ended in failure after a decade of Northern frustration and Southern hostility. The Great Society and the civil rights laws of the 1960s constitute the beginnings of a second attempt, and in the case of the Voting Rights Act, it was a significant success.

But that success hasn't fixed the problem, and many Americans have grown tired of trying to remedy the effects of racism. By striking down Section 4 of the VRA and ignoring the clear words of the Fifteenth Amendment, Roberts is elevating white America's racial fatigue into constitutional law.

Is this a backlash? I'm not sure. But between the Court's ruling on the VRA, the ongoing assaults on affirmative action, and the white public's belief in its own marginalization, I will say that, yet again, we have reached the limits of what this country will do to address the conditions of African Americans. Or, if not that, then we're taking another break—not a long one, let's hope—from grappling with the implications of our history.

> *"When talking about race there is always a part of me that feels as though I am perpetuating and legitimizing it, giving it the fixed status that it should never have. But then not to talk about race, or to try to ignore it, is not only impractical but also irresponsible."*

Even Talking About Race Brings About Unease

Sarah Ladipo Manyika

In the following viewpoint, Sarah Ladipo Manyika argues that America is not a post-racial society, pointing to fears she holds about her African-American son averting racist treatment by the police and others. In fact, she says, even simply holding an honest conversation about race seems to be too painful and fraught with complication. Sarah Ladipo Manyika holds a PhD from the University of California, Berkeley, and teaches literature at San Francisco State University. Her writing includes essays, academic papers, reviews, and short stories.

As you read, consider the following questions:

1. Why was the author taken aback at being asked how she identified racially?
2. Why did the author's husband instruct their son not to wear a hoodie?
3. What is the "minority mentality" mentioned in the article?

E arlier this year I decided to read Joe Brainard's cult classic, *I Remember*. The book had long intrigued me for I had heard that it was widely taught in creative writing courses and was a favorite of many authors, including several well-known authors whose work I admire. I was immediately drawn to Brainard's style, each line starting with the words "I remember." As I read it, I found myself jotting down remembrances of my own, complementing Brainard's memories of America with my memories of Nigeria.

I was enjoying this little book, reading it slowly, taking my time to appreciate the beauty and originality of the writing while remembering and reminiscing. It was a soothing and creative project until I came to this:

I remember feeling sorry for black people, not because I thought they were persecuted, but because I thought they were ugly.

I remember gasping.

I remember thinking, So this is what Zora Neale Hurston meant when she wrote, "I feel most colored when I am thrown against a sharp white background."

I remember ugly.

I remember not wanting to continue, but continuing all the same.

I remember it got worse several lines later when Brainard writes:

I remember speculating that probably someday science would come up with some sort of miracle cream that could bleach skin, and Negroes could become white.

I remember thinking, "So this is his solution, to make everyone white?"

I remember returning to [Paul] Auster's glowing preface.

I remember wondering if Auster felt anything close to my shock and sadness when reading those lines.

I remember not wanting to be disappointed in Auster.

I remember helping myself to some chocolate, and then to more.

I remember not being hungry, but eating as though starved.

I remember wondering if I was over-reacting.

I remember wondering if I was becoming consumed with race.

Thirteen years ago I wrote an essay entitled "Oyinbo," an autobiographical account of my personal experiences with race and racism. The narrative began with my countries of origin, Nigeria and England, and my parent's marriage—with my white mother who was disowned by her parents for choosing to marry a black man. The essay then wound its way through other places where I have lived or traveled—France, Zimbabwe, the U.S., and South Africa. I wrote of the social construction of race as found in America and Southern Africa and how these particular societal constructions of race were largely alien to me, having been raised in Nigeria. I also wrote of race in the U.K., which was partially eclipsed by the prevalence of social class, Britain's preferred mode of social segregation.

Before we were married, my husband asked me if I identified as "black." I remember thinking this an odd question. I thought it should be obvious that I identified as black even though I was, "technically," half black and half white. But right there, in the making of the half-black and half-white observation, was, perhaps, where some of my husband's concerns lay. What I didn't fully appreciate at the time was the history behind my husband's question. He had grown up in apartheid Rhodesia where he experienced segregation and racism very much as African Americans would have experienced it in 1960s America. It was important, therefore, for my husband to feel reassured, especially for the sake of any future children, that they would feel secure in their "race." I, in contrast, raised in Nigeria during the 1970s and '80s, did not grow up with race as a defining element of my upbringing or identity. Nigeria has no history of apartheid and no established tradition of societies structured along racial lines.

Twenty years of living in America has cured me of any whimsical notions I once held about the fluidity of racial categorization, and race now presents me with the following dilemma. When talking about race there is always a part of me that feels as though I am perpetuating and legitimizing it, giving it the fixed status that it should never have. But then not to talk about race, or to try to ignore it, is not only impractical but also irresponsible. I therefore try to follow what I feel James Baldwin so wisely advocates in many of his essays: to remain committed to the struggle against racism while trying to keep my heart free of hatred and despair. But with every passing year this has proven more difficult, even for someone who, by virtue of my gender, fair skin, and privileged socio-economic status is frequently cocooned from the nastier manifestations of racial discrimination. It has become increasingly hard to keep my heart free of despair while noticing the effects of discrimination, especially as it pertains to young black men in America. And since the birth of my son it has become increasingly personal. I ended "Oyinbo," wondering what my son's experience of race might be like when he became a young man:

> *My son Julian was pink with bright blue eyes when he was born, but now he has my coffee-and-cream colored complexion and dark brown eyes. Everyone says he, two years old, is cute—Oh, he's adorable! Oh, he's darling! What a cutie! He's such a looker!—It warms my heart but I wonder, when he's a teenager, tall, gangly, and black, what will people say?*

I have long known that my son would encounter racism, for even in the seemingly liberal, tolerant city of San Francisco where we live, we experienced several racial incidents in his early years.

I remember there was the woman at the playground who whispered to her white child not to touch my son because he was "dirty."

I remember our babysitter from Mexico, as she recalled this episode, crying and repeating, "He wasn't even sandy!"

I remember, on other occasions, biting my tongue—not because what I overheard of third-graders' fantasy play was meant to wound, but because it suggested that school or parents were neglecting to teach something essential about the history and legacy of race in America. "I'll be President Washington," announced my son's friend, placing a neck cushion on top of his straight brown hair to imitate a wig. "And you," he said, pointing to my son, "shall be my slave."

But even as I expected my son to encounter yet other forms of racism, I would never have predicted that he would come of age during a spate of highly publicized police killings of black men. Nor would I have thought that the words of civil rights activist Ella Baker would remain as relevant and urgent today as they were fifty years ago: "Until the killing of black men, black mothers' sons, becomes as important to the rest of the country as the killing of a white mother's sons—we who believe in freedom cannot rest until this happens." When I wrote "Oyinbo," I had hoped for progress, not regression, around issues of race, but instead, in the intervening years, economic inequalities between blacks and whites have risen, as have incarceration rates for black men and reports of police brutality against them.

It was in the context of the recent shootings of young black men that my family had the following conversation: We were walking home from dinner on a cold San Francisco night when my husband turned to our teenage son and said:

"I hope you don't wear your hoodie up at night, not when it's dark, and if we're not with you."

"No," our son replied. "Only if I'm alone. Or if I'm cold."

"But you shouldn't wear it at all," my husband insisted.

Our son sighed, unable to conceal his impatience.

"I'm serious about this one," his father repeated. "Okay?"

I sensed that if I could peek around the edge of our son's hoodie, I would have found him rolling his eyes in frustration. He was annoyed, and I didn't blame him. It is annoying to have to be so careful about how one dresses when other young people don't have to practice the same vigilance. Yet the tragic reality for young black men in this country is that the color of their skin marks them as threatening. The statistics are frightening—young black men in America are shot dead by police at twenty-one times the rate of young white men. There is nothing we can do to make our fifteen-year-old son any shorter than his current height of six foot three, but we can encourage him to dress in such a way that will, hopefully, make him appear less "threatening."

"It's just one of those sad things," said father to son.

In December, around the time of the grand jury decision not to indict the white officer in the choking death of Eric Garner, I remember talking to fellow black mothers about the ease with which others seemed able to go about the business of the holidays, without giving much thought to the pain and fear that gripped us. One friend of a friend, so afraid of what might happen to her teenage sons after a string of burglaries caused her neighbors to start warning against "anyone who looks out of place," decided to send photographs to all the neighbors so they would take note and really *see* her boys: so that they would know what her boys looked like: so that one day, should they be tempted to call the police on perceiving the threat of another "black male," they would instead see her sons for who they were—young men with names. I feel shocked when white friends are surprised to hear that one of my greatest fears for our son is that he will be stabbed or shot to death. Why, given all the statistics for young black males in America, do people continue to be surprised?

I sometimes hear friends complaining that it's too difficult to have an honest conversation about race in America, and from others I occasionally hear attempts to justify their fears of young black males. Recently, someone was brave enough to tell me that because she was once mugged by an African American man, in an elevator, she's now too scared to get into any elevator with a black man. She confessed she's fearful of black men. I told her I was sorry for what happened and empathized, for I too have experienced the terror of being attacked—but I did not tell her how profoundly her confession affected me. After all, it was white men who attacked me in broad daylight in the south of France, at a bus stop, where no passerby stopped to help me, yet I do not single out white men as the object of my fear. I couldn't bring myself to tell this woman how her confession had caused me to fall deeper into despair. I have known countless black men and boys in my life—my father, my husband, my brother, my son, my uncles, my godsons, my neighbors. Countless kind, responsible, flawed, ordinary, and extraordinary black men who have committed no acts of violence. And yet it felt somehow acceptable, even commonplace, for a white person to confess a fear of black men. I do not deny the fact that young black males have higher crime and incarceration rates, but the conversation cannot simply stop there. As this person went on detailing her fears, I could not help but think of Claudia Rankine's poem *Citizen: An American Lyric*. Line after line she writes "in memory" of young black men, concluding:

> because white men can't
>> police their imagination
>> black men are dying

As a parent of a young black man, I worry not only about my child's physical safety, but also about his emotional and mental well-being. Having grown up in Nigeria, I know what it's like to be free of the mental burden of race.

But I feel as though I have now become so burdened by race in America that I have acquired what the actor David Oyelowo refers to as a "minority mentality," a mentality that puts a damper on one's ambitions and outlook on life. Gone are the starry-eyed days of innocence. Now I see race in many things. The way black people are routinely called to one side at airports. The way that workers in fancy hotels, restaurants, and retail stores keep a wary eye on black people. Even the way that a white man the other day pulled up behind my car and started swearing at me and honking louder than I suspect he would have if I were not black, protesting that I was "stealing" the parking space that he had just done an illegal U turn for.

I see race where others do not, where race indeed might not be a factor, and I do not want this to be my son's experience. In my attempts not to overwhelm him with desperation, I find myself not wanting to dwell too much on all the news of racial violence and discrimination against black men. I want my son to be aware of racial prejudice, but not so much that he loses faith in the human race. There's a balance between mindfulness and despair that I'm not always sure I get right as a parent.

"What are your thoughts on race?" I asked my son one afternoon while writing this essay. I was trying to pitch the words just right, hoping that he wouldn't dismiss this as another annoying adult question. "How do you feel as a young black man in America?"

"That's too general," he replied.

"Do you worry about racism?"

"Um hmm," he said, shrugging his shoulders.

When I pushed him to explain what "um hmm" meant, he said he doesn't find that people are racist "on purpose" but "unconsciously," and that people's unconscious racism is what makes him a little bit "uneasy."

I probed further, "Does it feel burdensome being black?"

"In a joking way, for basketball," he smiled, and then, turning serious, he added that if he came from a lower-income family it would be different.

He left me with my thoughts, in the kitchen, but then called back:

"But yeah, on first instincts, the sound of the police is uneasy."

"The sound of what?" I asked, my heart lurching.

"The sound of police sirens," he called back. "It makes me feel uneasy."

My son's "unease" makes me uneasy. I know that for now, with nothing having happened to him directly, or anyone close to him, he remains philosophical and is even able to joke about racial stereotyping. But how long does this "relative innocence" last? "By the time you hear the next pop, the funk shall be within you," flows Kendrick Lamar in "King Kunta," one of my son's favorite songs.

A few months ago my son drew a self-portrait for his high school art class. He worked studiously on it for several days and when he showed it to me, I saw a confident young man at home in his skin. It took me back to a recent family vacation, where I stood in the Museu Picasso with my son, both of us admiring Picasso's self-portrait of 1896, drawn when he was roughly the same age my son is now. Filled with a mother's pride, I emailed a copy of my son's art to my parents. While I did not expect anyone else to see the Picasso, the Elizabeth Catlett, or the Bruce Onobrakpeya that I could see in my son's self-portrait, I was not expecting the first line of my mother's email response to be, "Don't let the police get this!" Her response reminded me of how others might see my son, a hall-of-mirrors angle reinforced by the constant display of police sketches of young black suspects. This was the view I didn't normally see, that I didn't want to see. Like Brainard's "ugly," it made me gasp. Made me ache. I went back to my son's self-portrait and stared at it for a long time.

I couldn't bring myself to tell my mother how her response had affected me until I had written this essay—more proof of how difficult it is to talk about race even with those closest and dearest. My mother meant no harm by what she wrote. I knew this, but what she had presumed I would understand as her dry Yorkshire humor was completely lost to me in the context of race in America.

Another book that I picked up at the beginning of the year was Deborah Levy's *Things I Don't Want to Know*. This gem, written by a white, Jewish woman who grew up in South Africa and England, is a thoughtful, feminist response to George Orwell's essay "Why I Write."

I remember Levy asking, "What do we do with knowledge that we cannot bear to live with? What do we do with the things we do not want to know?"

I remember her implied response—one writes about them.

I remember this as young black men across America are killing each other and being killed by police officers that are supposed to protect them.

I remember this as society fails to address wealth and class inequalities and thereby returns the vast majority of black people in America to a new form of servitude.

These are things I don't want to know, but they are there. Pulling at me.

And my little boy is becoming a man.

And I worry.

> "Any time an individual is granted preferential treatment based on race, opportunities are denied to others who may be just as qualified or needy but who simply have the "wrong" skin color or are the wrong gender."

Affirmative Action is Racial Discrimination

Jennifer Gratz

In the following viewpoint, Jennifer Gratz argues against the benefits of affirmative action. The purpose of offering special treatment in hiring or college admissions is to make up for past discrimination and to foster diversity. However, she believes, racial preferences often stigmatize people who earned their accomplishments without special treatment. Affirmative action is a form of discrimination against those who also have worked hard against obstacles. Jennifer Gratz is founder and chief executive officer of the XIV Foundation, an organization dedicated to teaching the personal and societal advantages of fair and equal treatment, and lead plaintiff in the landmark Supreme Court case challenging the University of Michigan's use of racial preferences in undergraduate admissions.

"Discriminating Toward Equality: Affirmative Action and the Diversity Charade," Jennifer Gratz, Heritage Foundation, February 27, 2014. Reprinted by permission.

As you read, consider the following questions:

1. What is the purpose of affirmative action policies in employment and college admissions?
2. Why have many states passed laws banning affirmative action?
3. How can colleges and workplaces achieve their goals of diversity without resorting to affirmative action?

Affirmative action was intended to ensure that all Americans are treated without regard to race. Today, public officials and educators justify using special treatment based on race to make up for past discrimination and to foster diversity. Stories of the victims of racial preferences, however, reveal the hidden consequences of these well-intentioned efforts to manufacture racial balance. Racial preferences are a form of discrimination, and they stigmatize those whose accomplishments are not due to such preferences. Race-based discrimination policies continue to undermine the American Dream, and the only way to end the vicious cycle of discrimination is to ensure that fair and equal treatment for everyone is a reality, not just a talking point.

On October 15, 2013, the topic of affirmative action once again came before the United States Supreme Court. This time, the debate over race-based preferences came to the Court via *Schuette v. Coalition to Defend Affirmative Action*, a case that challenges Michigan's constitutional ban on government racial preference policies. Seven other states have passed similar measures ending race-based policies, and the Court's ruling in *Schuette* will have national implications for the future of affirmative action and the pursuit of equal treatment under the law for every individual.

Origins of Affirmative Action

The term "affirmative action" was first used by President John F. Kennedy in 1961 when he issued Executive Order 10925, requiring government contractors to "take affirmative action to ensure that applicants are employed, and that employees are treated during employment, *without regard* to their race, creed, color, or national origin."[1] Today, America's understanding of the term has changed dramatically.

After the passage of the 1964 Civil Rights Act, Kennedy's "without regard" standard was transformed into policies that encouraged public officials, educators, and administrators to actively treat people *with* regard to race. Relying on allowances in Titles II and VII of the Civil Rights Act, federal, state, and local governments instituted special racial boosts and preferences with the goal of increasing minority representation in education and employment. Over the years, this special treatment based on race has been justified as remedying past discrimination, expanding opportunities for the underprivileged, and, more recently, fostering diversity. Thus, "affirmative action" today is an innocuous-sounding phrase for what are really racial preferences.

Michigan's Ban on Preferential Treatment

In 2006, Michigan voters passed Proposal 2, also known as the Michigan Civil Rights Initiative (MCRI), amending their state constitution to end preferential treatment based on race, ethnicity, or gender at public institutions. The law's goal was equal treatment under the law, and the language of the amendment reflected that simple message: "The State shall not discriminate against or grant preferential treatment to any group or individual on the basis of race, sex, color, ethnicity or national origin in the operation of public employment, public education or public contracting."[2]

Immediately after Election Day, the initiative's leading opponent, the radical Coalition to Defend Affirmative Action, Integration and Immigrant Rights and Fight for Equality By Any Means Necessary (BAMN), filed a lawsuit challenging the constitutionality of requiring equal treatment in public education. As a result of this requirement, BAMN argued, the MCRI violates the Fourteenth Amendment of the U.S. Constitution. BAMN contends that the legal impact and political restructuring of banning preferences at the constitutional level fall wholly upon, and thus target, powerless minorities. Only the University of Michigan Board of Regents has the authority to decide whether or not a person's skin color can be considered in making admissions decisions, according to BAMN, and the people of Michigan had no right to choose equal treatment as a matter of state law.

At the core of BAMN's position is the belief not only that it is unconstitutional to treat people without regard to race, but also that the fundamental protections of the Fourteenth Amendment extend only to certain minorities. In fact, an attorney for BAMN, Shanta Driver, made that argument before the Supreme Court during the *Schuette* oral arguments. When Justice Antonin Scalia asked Ms. Driver whether she could cite any case in support of her racial view of the Fourteenth Amendment, she responded, "No case of yours."[3]

While the Supreme Court has heard several cases on this issue, it has shied away from striking down the use of race across the board. Instead the Court has restricted the use of such race-based policies to "achieve diversity" while encouraging states to transition to race-neutral alternatives to meet that goal. As a result, states have emerged as the frontier for pursuing equal treatment under the law.

Much progress has been made over the past 15 years. California, Washington, Florida, Michigan, Nebraska, Arizona, New Hampshire, and Oklahoma have ended the public use of racial preferences through various means: executive order, legislation, referendum, and constitutional amendment by citizen initiatives. The Court will soon decide whether or not states have the right to continue moving in this direction.

Negative Consequences of Affirmative Action

The *Schuette* case is important, and so is changing the law, but even if the Supreme Court decided today that racial preferences are unconstitutional, these policies would linger because public officials and school administrators continue to support them. In fact, they will continue to direct policy decisions until individuals are confronted with the moral and practical costs of treating people differently based on skin color or their ethnic heritage. It is easy to engage this subject in the realm of laws, statistics, and court cases, but the real people who are adversely affected by these policies are often overlooked. The stories of the victims of racial preferences reveal the hidden consequences of efforts to equalize outcomes and manufacture an ever-changing ideal of racial balance.

When it comes to typical "reverse discrimination" cases, many people know high-profile stories like mine and that of Frank Ricci. For instance, my story made national headlines when I challenged the University of Michigan's decision to use skin color as the primary basis for rejecting my application for admission.

At the time of my application, the university reviewed applications submitted by black, Native American, and Hispanic applicants under one standard and those submitted by everyone else under a much higher standard.[4] The school later claimed to simplify the admissions process by using a point system and automatically awarding an extra 20 points (out of 100) to select minorities. By comparison, a perfect SAT score earned an applicant only 12 points. Thus, even though I had good grades and a host of extracurricular activities, the university rejected my application because I had the wrong skin color. My case, *Gratz v. Bollinger*,[5] ultimately went before the Supreme Court, and in 2003, the Court ruled that racial discrimination had indeed taken place.

In another high-profile case, Frank Ricci, a firefighter for the city of New Haven, Connecticut, took and passed the exam for promotion to lieutenant. The results of this test, however, were discarded by the city because no black firefighters scored high enough to be considered for the open positions. Ricci and 17 others (including a Hispanic applicant) sued New Haven for reverse discrimination, and in the 2009 *Ricci v. DeStefano* decision,[6] the Supreme Court ruled in their favor.

Frank and I both worked hard and expected to be judged on our character and merit. Instead, despite our qualifications, we faced rejection because of an obsession with racial policies.

Proponents of reverse discrimination often argue that only privileged white individuals have any reason to oppose the use of racial preferences. These diversity engineers believe the benefits of expanding opportunities to certain minorities far outweigh the costs of using race to treat people differently. However, the personal stories of those who have been adversely affected by these policies—both the traditional victims and even the supposed beneficiaries—paint a very different picture. The following are just a few of them.[7]

The Stigma of Affirmative Action

Ashley graduated from high school at 16 years of age with a 4.3 GPA and scored a 32 on the ACT.[8] She was active in numerous extracurricular activities and, not surprisingly, was accepted into every college to which she applied. Ashley did not want racial admissions boosts, and she did not need them. She knew, however, that she would get them anyway because she happened to be black. Despite her hard work and impressive accomplishments, she feared ever having a bad day or getting an answer wrong in class lest her peers think she got accepted only because of her skin color.

The use of race-conscious admissions policies at her university saddled Ashley with an unwanted stigma based on her skin color. It reinforced stereotypes of inequality and special treatment, forcing her constantly to feel the need to prove that she deserved to be in the classroom. Rather than helping Ashley, racial preferences obscured the legitimacy of her achievements. She wanted to be judged as an individual; instead, she worked twice as hard to overcome being judged for her skin color.

Patricia worked hard and made many sacrifices to achieve her dream of being a police officer. However, even after years on the job and having received many commendations, she still felt that she had to work twice as hard as her male colleagues to demonstrate that she deserved to be there. As a woman, Patricia struggled to overcome the stigma of gender preferences. Over and over again, she worked to prove that the promotions she received were the result of merit, not a diversity quota. The shadow of affirmative action diminished her accomplishments in the eyes of colleagues and robbed her of the honor and satisfaction she deserved. She did not need affirmative action, but she still suffered its consequences.

Recently, the University of Michigan's Black Student Union received national attention when its "Being Black at the University of Michigan" hashtag went viral on Twitter. Hundreds of students joined in to share the "unique experiences of being black at Michigan."[9] The vast majority of the comments were negative, and almost every single one of the students who commented expressed frustration with being treated differently because of his or her skin color. The students' demand that they be treated as unique individuals—instead of as token members of racial or ethnic groups—was striking, and it highlighted the fact that putting people in boxes and discriminating based on appearance is demeaning, harmful, and wrong. Is it any less so when it is done by public officials and administrators?

The "Wrong" Kind of Minority

David, a student living in Los Angeles, wanted to attend the University of California, Los Angeles, but was rejected despite excellent grades and test scores.[10] David happened to be Vietnamese and was held to a much higher admission standard because of his ethnicity. Even being a minority applicant won him no favor in the system of discrimination for the sake of diversity. In the interest of maintaining a diverse campus, the university chose to limit the number of high-performing Asian enrollees. He was told he should accept discrimination for the "common good" and that he could always attend another elite school. For David, however, racial discrimination forced him to choose between taking care of his immobile grandmother and moving out-of-state to further his education.

Barbara Grutter, the mother of two sons, applied to the University of Michigan Law School in 1996.[11] Before applying, she had started a successful business, had graduated from Michigan State with a 3.8 GPA and high honors, and had scored 161 on the LSAT. She also happened to be white. The law school initially placed Barbara on their waiting list but later rejected her. Only 20 percent of white and Asian students with similar marks got into the school; however, "underrepresented" minorities with the same grades had a 100 percent acceptance rate.

Why the disparity? The law school gave preferences to certain applicants based on skin color. Grutter decided to sue, and in the course of the court hearings and testimony, it became clear that race accounted for well over a quarter of applicants' admission scores. Unfortunately, in 2003, the Supreme Court, in *Grutter v. Bollinger*, upheld the school's racially discriminatory policies as necessary for achieving the goals of a diverse campus.[12] The Court's holding was based on the flimsy rationale that because the preferences were not codified into a point system, they were permissible as part of a "holistic" admissions process.

Barbara entered the workforce in the 1970s along with many other women "empowered and emboldened by the belief that equal opportunity meant that it was illegal to judge anyone on the basis of race, gender, or anything else that has nothing to do with one's abilities."[13] She feared this newfound opportunity would prove illusory and that it could be "pulled back" at any moment, which is ultimately what happened—because of her race.

Experts insisted that racial preferences and the pursuit of diversity were good for Barbara and society as a whole. She could always attend another law school, they argued. Yet none of these experts discussed the fact that Barbara was only interested in attending a well-respected law school and, as a mother of two young children, was unable to move out-of-state to attend other schools. The University of Michigan was her only real option, but she was denied admission because of her race.

Katuria Smith grew up in poverty.[14] She was born when her mother was 17, had an alcoholic father and stepfather, dropped out of high school, and survived on any menial job she could find. By the time she turned 21 years old, Katuria was desperate to escape poverty, so she took night classes at a community college paralegal program while juggling jobs during the day. She graduated and enrolled in the University of Washington where she earned a degree.

With her 3.65 GPA and LSAT score of 165, Katuria applied to the University of Washington School of Law. Considering her background, she expected to be admitted. Instead, her application was rejected.

In order to bolster campus diversity, the university used race as a factor in determining whom to admit to its law school, maintaining separate admissions standards and procedures for minority applicants. The dean later admitted that with her story and qualifications, Katuria would have been accepted had she been a member of a "preferred" racial group.[15] The university claimed they employed a "holistic" approach in the admissions process, but even Katuria's incredible life story of overcoming remarkable hurdles was not enough to make up for the fact that she was not the right color. In the end, a "holistic" admission proved to be mostly about race.

"Equal Pay for Equal Work"

After concerns arose about unequal compensation among white male, female, and minority faculty, Northern Arizona University set out to implement a "pay equity" plan. The university used a computer program to calculate appropriate salary ranges for each professor and awarded one-time pay raises to 64 white female and 27 minority professors who were assessed as underpaid.

Interestingly, the study also ranked 192 white male professors as underpaid, but they were frozen out of any salary increases.[16] It turns out that equalizing pay was not about "equal pay for equal work"; rather, the school wanted to use skin color and gender to manufacture results. These professors were treated as pawns in an ugly game of racial and gender "balancing," but after years of legal battles, a federal court called it what it was: discrimination.[17]

An Honest Discussion About Race and Equality

Larry, the owner of a popular bar and restaurant in Detroit, used to own several hair salons around the time the *Gratz* and *Grutter* cases were being argued before the Supreme Court.[18] There was a full crowd in one of the salons on the day that a television in the salon carried a news report about my fight to be treated equally at the University of Michigan. Larry remembers his wife loudly remarking, "Well, why shouldn't she be treated equally?" This sparked a discussion among the crowd. Larry, his wife, and much of their clientele happened to be black. Whether or not they agreed with racial preferences, they had serious conversations about the fairness of these policies.

Questioning the merits of treating people differently based on race is far more common than the supporters of racial preferences would like the public to believe. Friends, families, and colleagues are talking honestly about race and equality. Unfortunately, race-based politics and political correctness keep these honest discussions in the shadows.

The Double Standard

Lee Bollinger is a prominent supporter of racial preferences and a self-proclaimed champion of diversity and equal opportunity. He was president of the University of Michigan when Barbara and I filed our lawsuits, and he publicly supported the university's right to use race-based preferences throughout the legal proceedings. To him, a 20 percent boost for race meant "one of many factors," and selectively distributing special treatment based on race was consistent with equal protection under the law.

Now the president of Columbia University, Mr. Bollinger recently dealt with a new discrimination matter—a "whites only" scholarship fund established by a wealthy divorcee days before her death in 1920.[19] Bollinger is seeking a court order to lift the

AFFIRMATIVE ACTION LEVELS THE PLAYING FIELD

As President Lyndon Johnson said in 1965, "You do not take a person who, for years, has been hobbled by chains and liberate him, bring him up to the starting line of a race and then say you are free to compete with all the others, and still just believe that you have been completely fair."

President Johnson's speech eloquently stated the rationale behind the contemporary use of affirmative action programs to achieve equal opportunity, especially in the fields of employment and higher education.

The emphasis is on opportunity: affirmative action programs are meant to break down barriers, both visible and invisible, to level the playing field, and to make sure everyone is given an equal break. They are not meant to guarantee equal results—but instead proceed on the common-sense notion that if equality of opportunity were a reality, African Americans, women, people with disabilities and other groups facing discrimination would be fairly represented in the nation's work force and educational institutions.

[...]

The continuing need for affirmative action is demonstrated by the data. For example, the National Asian and Pacific American Legal Consortium reports that although white men make up only 48% of the college-educated workforce, they hold over 90% of the top jobs in the news media, 96% of CEO positions, 86% of law firm partnerships, and 85% of tenured college faculty positions.

"Affirmative Action." The Leadership Conference.

race restrictions because of the ugliness of discrimination, but he has remained silent on the long list of scholarships Columbia promotes only for "students of color." In the eyes of Bollinger and those who agree with his position, preferential treatment counts as discrimination only when the race in question is not currently favored by the government or those in academia's ivory towers.

President Obama on Affirmative Action

When the Michigan Civil Rights Initiative appeared on the ballot in 2006, then-Senator Barack Obama recorded a radio ad urging viewers to vote against it.[20] He insisted that by not allowing policies that grant special treatment based on skin color, Michigan would undermine equal opportunity and reverse racial progress.

Just a year later, ABC News' George Stephanopoulos asked Senator Obama whether his daughters should receive special treatment because of their race when applying to college.[21] Obama said his two daughters "should probably be treated by any admissions officer as folks who are pretty advantaged"—a subtle acknowledgement of the absurdity of using race to determine preferential treatment. While his daughters may share the same skin color as a child in inner-city Chicago, their backgrounds are worlds apart. In today's increasingly pluralistic society, race usually does not—and certainly should not—determine what obstacles individuals have had to overcome or advantages they have received.

A Legacy of Discrimination

There are four important lessons to draw from the stories recounted above.

Racial preferences are a form of discrimination. Any time an individual is granted preferential treatment based on race, opportunities are denied to others who may be just as qualified or needy but who simply have the "wrong" skin color or are the wrong gender. The government's preference for one race (or gender or ethnicity) over another is the very definition of discrimination. Regardless of intentions, such policies create new injustices with new victims. No one—white, black, Asian, Latino, Native American, or any other color or ethnicity—should be turned away from education, scholarships, jobs, contracts, or promotions because they have the "wrong" skin color. This kind of discrimination was wrong 50 years ago, and it is still wrong today.

Racial preferences rob recipients of the pride of ownership in their accomplishments. When individuals of a certain race are selected to receive special treatment, those individuals must struggle against the idea that their skin color rather than merit is behind their success. Indeed, the achievements of people like Ashley, who did not need or want preferences, will forever be judged through the lens of racial preferences.

The values of the diversity movement are only skin deep. Proponents of these reverse discrimination policies refuse to treat people as individuals. Instead, they rely on discriminatory stereotypes and gross generalizations to label, judge, and group people based on race, gender, and ethnicity. Individuals are reduced to a skin color or gender type because diversity's champions have little patience for the actual work needed to promote real diversity. Ask a university president how many black students are on campus, and he or she will be able to provide the number on the spot. But ask about the number of musicians, conservatives, liberals, libertarians, or students from single-parent homes, and he or she will be at a loss to provide any meaningful statistics. Real diversity is found in the wealth of experience, talents, perspectives, and interests of unique individuals. People of the same race do not all think alike.

Race-based policies force people to make decisions and judgments that do not reflect how people live their lives. The average person thinks very little about race on a daily basis, yet the diversity culture and racial preference policies insist that race is the centerpiece of almost every issue, work environment, and educational experience. People are constantly forced to describe themselves by checking a box or choosing a label from a list of predetermined and frequently artificial categories. From an early age, children are taught not to judge a person based on appearance, but when they grow older, they learn that this is exactly what is happening and being encouraged all around them.

America is ready to move beyond race. However, if the government and public institutions continue to divide the country by ethnicity and race, the goal of a color-blind society will remain beyond our reach. Policies that promote race-based discrimination continue to undermine the American Dream, and the only way to end the vicious cycle of discrimination is to ensure that fair and equal treatment for everyone is a reality, not just a talking point.

References

[1] Exec. Order No. 10925, 26 Fed. Reg. 1977 (Mar. 8, 1961) (emphasis added).

[2] Mich. Const. art. I, § 26, cl. 2.

[3] Transcript of Oral Argument at 42, Schuette v. Coalition to Defend Affirmative Action (No. 12-682),available at http://www.supremecourt.gov/oral_arguments/argument_transcripts/12-682_l537.pdf.

[4] Center for Individual Rights, Charting Racial Discrimination, http://www.cir-usa.org/cases/michigan_lsa_charts.html (last visited Feb. 7, 2014) (the guidelines used by the University of Michigan's undergraduate admissions office).

[5] 539 U.S. 244 (2003).

[6] 557 U.S. 557 (2009).

[7] Some names have been changed to protect privacy.

[8] Videotape: Adam Abraham, An Act of Courage (American Civil Rights Coalition 2004) (on file with author). Ashley is featured in this video.

[9] Rhonesha Byng, #BBUM Hashtag Sparks Dialogue About Diversity at the University of Michigan, Huffington Post, Nov. 20, 2013, available at http://www.huffingtonpost.com/2013/11/20/bbum-university-of-michigan-black-students_n_4310790.html?ncid=txtlnkushpmg00000038.

[10] Interview with Jennifer Gratz.

[11] News Conference, Center for Individual Rights, Supreme Court Affirmative Action Cases (Mar. 31, 2003), available at http://www.c-spanvideo.org/program/CourtAf.

[12] 539 U.S. 306 (2003).

[13] News Conference, supra note 11.

[14] Center for Individual Rights, Smith v. University of Washington, http://www.cir-usa.org/cases/smith.html (last visited Feb. 7, 2014) (a compilation of documents related to Katuria's lawsuit).

[15] Nat Hentoff, Katuria Smith Goes to Court, Village Voice, July 8, 1998, available at http://www.cir-usa.org/articles/140.html.

[16] White Males Fight the Freeze, Times Higher Education, Dec. 4, 1995, available athttp://www.timeshighereducation.co.uk/news/white-males-fight-the-freeze/96258.article.

[17] Piper Fogg, Northern Arizona U. Violated Rights of White Male Professors, Judge Rules, Chronicle of Higher Education, July 16, 2004, available at http://chronicle.com/article/Northern-Arizona-U-Violated/5861.

[18] Interview with Jennifer Gratz in Detroit, Michigan (July 2013).

[19] Sharyn Jackson, Whites-only Scholarship at Columbia Challenged, USA Today, May 15, 2013, available athttp://www.usatoday.com/story/news/nation/2013/05/15/whites-only-scholarship-challenged/2164815/.

[20] Stephen Hayes, The Race Minefield, Weekly Standard, Mar. 10, 2008, available athttp://www.weeklystandard.com/Content/Public/Articles/000/000/014/823xthib.asp?pg=1#.

[21] Eugene Robinson, A Question of Race v. Class, Wash. Post, May 15, 2007, available athttp://www.washingtonpost.com/wp-dyn/content/article/2007/05/14/AR2007051401233.html.

> *"You see, it is a revolutionary act to be a Black girl or woman who loves herself in a world where she is reminded that she should not."*

Despite Oppression, Black Women are Thriving

Lakisha Watson-Moore

In the following viewpoint, Lakisha Watson-Moore argues that Black girls and women face obstacles in America that many white people don't realize or understand. They are often criticized for their appearance instead of celebrated for the features that make them unique and beautiful. They have been systematically discriminated against, and suffer from social, political, and economic inequalities. Despite these obstacles, women such as First Lady Michelle Obama are proving that black women can overcome stereotypes to achieve success. Lakisha Wastson-Moore is a blogger at Bougie Black Girl, an online forum for black women.

As you read, consider the following questions:

1. According to the author, what are some of the stereotypes that many Americans believe about black women?
2. According to the author, what are some of the ways in which black women have altered their appearance to fit into the white world?
3. Why does the author think that it is a revolutionary act for black women and girls to love themselves?

Dear White folks who are mad at Michelle Obama for saying Black Girls Rock,
I think I know why you are mad. You are not used to seeing other women rock because for centuries you've been told that only you do. Perhaps it is jarring to see that other people exist beyond being your sidekicks, model minorities, imaginary friends and false stereotypes that promote the myth of your supremacy. You see, unlike you, for 400 years Black women and girls have been told we don't rock. Heck we've been told a lot worse. The thing is you've never known how it feels to be a Black woman in America. So this post is my meager attempt to show you.

1. Imagine how it feels being told every single day that because of the amount of melanin in your skin, the world instantly assumes you are hood, ghetto, uneducated, immoral, lazy, a leech on government and violent.
2. Imagine knowing that these ideas are lies and regardless of who you are and what you do, you can't change that lie because you don't control the image.
3. Imagine being told that your God-given tresses are ugly, unprofessional, unmanageable and bad hair.
4. Imagine having to spend thousands each year on chemicals to straighten your hair, without knowing the health risks of burning and scarring our scalps just to be accepted.
5. Imagine not being the standard of beauty within your race.

6. Imagine watching shows, reading articles and hearing new studies where people say you are not marriage material simply based on the color of your skin.

7. Imagine people calling their racist stereotypes about you a preference.

8. Imagine knowing that some employers will not look at your resume because you have a Black sounding name.

9. Imagine hearing White women complain about making $.77 to a White man's dollar when Black women only make $.64 and people rarely talk about it.

10. Imagine being told that regardless of your hopes and dreams that Black women are doomed to be the backbone of your race.

11. Imagine the burden of constantly representing your race and then being the blame for your race's ills when one person out of millions of Black people makes a mistake.

12. Imagine how it feels when people of your race make rap songs calling you b****s, hoes and anything but the child of god.

13. Imagine Black celebrities openly stating that they won't date you because of the texture of your hair, the darkness of your skin and because you are Black. But in the next breath they will use emotional blackmail because if you do not support their movie, album or book, Hollywood won't hire Black leads.

14. Imagine then marching, fighting and dying for the Black men, White women and others who ignore you because you are a Black woman.

15. Imagine knowing that those same people will never march, fight or even die for you. They'd prefer to ignore you.

16. Imagine having non-Blacks mock 400 years of rape, murder, broken families, state supported terrorism against you, income inequality and your ability to survive it all by calling themselves "a strong independent Black woman."

17. Imagine how it feels when your existence becomes a joke made by Black male comedians to their White audiences.

18. Imagine how it feels to have to wait over 30 years to finally see a Black woman lead on TV. This time she wasn't a slave, on drugs, a prostitute, a maid, struggling or a big mamma, with superhuman strength who was sassy and angry, but content with her pain because she's overly religious.

19. Imagine having those new images questioned because all Black women are supposed to be angry, not classically beautiful, are told there are too many on TV and are supposed to be a stereotype.

20. Imagine how it feels to know that even though your family has been here for 400 years, your history is not considered standard American history. It is only recognized in February and even during the month of February being told that Black history heroes are all Black men.

21. Imagine how it feels to be ignored in America when 64,000 of our daughters, mothers and sisters are missing.

22. Imagine how it feels to be one of the 40-60% of Black women and girls who are sexually abused by the time they reach 18 years old.

23. Imagine how it feels to be suspended from school at a higher rate than your peers of other races who commit the same infractions.

24. Imagine how it feels to receive a higher prison sentence for the same crimes than your female peers simply because you have Black skin.

25. Imagine being told you are the blame for the country's social ills when statistics show you are not.

26. Imagine having to write this post and explaining to someone whose image dominates the media and race controls the political, social and economic spheres why Black girls rock.

27. Imagine having you discount everything I said because deep down, you like things just the way they are.

After everything I have said (and I could go on), if Black women and girls being told by another Black woman that they rock offends you, check yourself and your insecurities. Instead of having a problem with Black Girls Rock, have a problem with the White supremacy that constantly tries to remind Black women and girls that we don't. Direct your energy towards a world that refuses to recognize our collective humanity. If you did, we wouldn't have to constantly remind Black women and girls that we are powerful, beautiful, worthy and full of love. You see, it is a revolutionary act to be a Black girl or woman who loves herself in a world where she is reminded that she should not. Even with every odd stacked against us, Black women and girls are thriving. So yes, Black girls do rock.

Periodical and Internet Sources Bibliography

The following articles have been selected to supplement the diverse views presented in this chapter.

Derrick Clifton, "10 Simple Ways White People Can Step Up to Fight Everyday Racism," *Mic*, September 4, 2014.

Yessenia Funes, "Finally, the U.S. Steps Closer to Racial Healing with a National Truth and Reconciliation Commission," *Yes! Magazine*, April 13, 2016.

Nikole Hannah-Jones, "What Abigail Fisher's Affirmative Action Case was Really About," ProPublica, June 23, 2016.

Greg Jones, "Sorry, Everyone, America Isn't That Racist," *Federalist*, July 7, 2015.

Peniel Joseph, "Obama's Legacy," *Washington Post*, April 22, 2016.

Chris Mooney, "The Science of Why Cops Shoot Young Black Men," *Mother Jones*, December 1, 2014.

Sarah Ladipo Manyika, "Coming of Age in the Time of the Hoodie," On the Commons, June 15, 2015.

Sean McElwee, "The Hidden Racism of Young White Americans," PBS.org, March 24, 2015.

Sergio Munoz, "Myths and Facts about Affirmative Action, Higher Education, and the Constitution," *Media Matters*, October 9, 2012.

Latonya Pennington, "Despite Legacy of Racism, Black Women Rock On," *Establishment*, July 2, 2016.

Valerie Strauss, "How 'Colorblind' Education Reform Policies Actually Ignore Racial Inequality," *Washington Post*, April 9, 2014.

For Further Discussion

Chapter 1

1. What messages do some African Americans have to give white Americans about what it is like to be black in America?
2. How do the opinions about race relations in the United States today differ between white and nonwhite Americans?
3. Do you think that then-Senator Barack Obama would agree with Ta-Nehisi Coates's view of race and inequality in the United States?

Chapter 2

1. What impact does the media have on forming opinions about race and inequality in the United States?
2. Do you agree with many social science professionals that race is a human construct?
3. Do you think it is possible to be color-blind when it comes to race in America today?

Chapter 3

1. What has been the impact of mass incarceration on communities of color?
2. What are some of the complaints that black Americans have about the way their communities are policed?
3. Why are students of color more often disciplined in schools today?

Chapter 4

1. What are some challenges that women of color face in the United States today?
2. What can Americans do to have an honest discussion about racial healing?
3. What is your opinion of the goals and success of affirmative action in college admissions?

Organizations to Contact

The editors have compiled the following list of organizations concerned with the issues debated in this book. The descriptions are derived from materials provided by the organizations. All have publications or information available for interested readers. The list was compiled on the date of publication of the present volume; the information provided here may change. Be aware that many organizations take several weeks or longer to respond to inquiries, so allow as much time as possible.

American Civil Rights Institute
PO Box 188350, Sacramento, CA 95818
phone: (916) 444-2278
website: acri.org
email: feedback@acri.org

The American Civil Rights Institute (ACRI) is a nationally recognized civil rights organization created to educate the public about racial and gender preferences. It was established by Ward Connerly and Dusty Rhodes in 1996. ACRI assists state grassroots organizations and publishes the online newsletter, the *Egalitarian*.

Amnesty International USA
5 Penn Plaza, New York, N.Y. 10001
phone: (212) 807-8400
website: www.amnestyusa.org
email: aimember@aiusa.org

Amnesty International is a global movement of people fighting injustice and promoting human rights. They work to protect people wherever justice, freedom, truth, and dignity are denied. Currently the world's largest grassroots human rights organization, they investigate and expose abuses, educate and mobilize the public, and help transform societies to create a safer, more just world.

Center for Constitutional Rights (CCR)
666 Broadway, 7th Floor, New York, N.Y. 10012
phone: (212) 614-6464
website: www.ccrjustice.org

The Center for Constitutional Rights is dedicated to advancing and protecting the rights guaranteed by the US Constitution and the Universal Declaration of Human Rights. Founded in 1966 by attorneys who represented civil rights movements in the South, CCR is a nonprofit legal and educational organization committed to the creative use of law as a positive force for social change.

Center for Equal Opportunity
7700 Leesburg Pike, Suite 231, Falls Church, VA 22043
phone: (703) 442-0066
website: www.ceousa.org

The Center for Equal Opportunity is the nation's only conservative think tank devoted to issues of race and ethnicity. It works to promote a color-blind society, one within which race and skin color are no longer an issue.

Harvard Project on American Indian Economic Development
79 John F. Kennedy Street, Cambridge, MA 02138
phone: (617) 495-1480
website: www.hpaied.org
email: hpaied@hks.harvard.edu

The Harvard Project aims to understand and foster the conditions under which sustained, self-determined social and economic development is achieved among American Indian nations through applied research and service.

The Leadership Conference on Civil and Human Rights
1629 K Street NW, 10th Floor, Washington, DC 20006
phone: (202) 466-3311
website: http://www.civilrights.org

The Leadership Conference on Civil and Human Rights is the nation's oldest, largest, and most diverse coalition of organizations committed to the protection of civil and human rights in the United States. It represents people of color, women, labor unions, persons with disabilities, older Americans, major religious groups, gays and lesbians, and civil liberties and human rights groups.

National Association for the Advancement of Colored People (NAACP)
4805 Mount Hope Drive, Baltimore, MD 21215
phone: (877) 622-2798
website: www.naacp.org

The mission of the National Association for the Advancement of Colored People is to ensure the political, educational, social, and economic equality of rights of all persons and to eliminate race-based discrimination.

National Urban League
120 Wall Street, New York, NY 10005
phone: (212) 558-5300
website: www.nul.org

The National Urban League is a civil rights organization dedicated to economic empowerment in order to elevate the standard of living in historically underserved urban communities. The National Urban League spearheads the efforts of its local affiliates through the development of programs, public policy research, and advocacy.

The Prejudice Institute
2743 Maryland Avenue, Baltimore, MD 21218
phone: (410) 243-6987
website: prejudiceinstitute.org
email: prejudiceinstitute@gmail.com

The Prejudice Institute/Center for the Applied Study of Ethnoviolence is a national research center concerned with violence and intimidation motivated by prejudice. It conducts research, supplies information on model programs and legislation, and provides education and training to combat prejudicial violence. The Prejudice Institute publishes research reports, bibliographies, and the quarterly newsletter *Forum*.

Southern Poverty Law Center (SPLC)

400 Washington Avenue, Montgomery, AL 36104
phone: (334) 956-8200
website: https://www.splcenter.org

The Southern Poverty Law Center (SPLC) litigates civil cases to protect the rights of poor people, particularly when those rights are threatened by white supremacist groups. The affiliated Klanwatch Project and the Militia Task Force collect data on white supremacist groups and militias. SPLC publishes numerous books and reports as well as the monthly *Klanwatch Intelligence Report*.

US Commission on Civil Rights

624 Ninth Street NW, Washington, DC 20425
phone: (202) 376-7700
website: www.usccr.gov

The Civil Rights Act of 1957 created the US Commission on Civil Rights. Since then, Congress has reauthorized or extended the legislation creating the commission several times; the last reauthorization was in 1994 by the Civil Rights Commission Amendments Act of 1994. Established as an independent, bipartisan, fact-finding federal agency, its mission is to inform the development of national civil rights policy and enhance enforcement of federal civil rights laws.

Bibliography of Books

Eduardo Bonilla-Silva, *Racism without Racists: Color-Blind Racism and the Persistence of Racial Inequality in America.* Lanham, MD: Rowman & Littlefield Publishers, Inc., 2014.

Devon W. Carbado and Mitu Gulati, *Acting White? Rethinking Race in Post-Racial America.* New York: Oxford University Press, 2015.

Jeff Chang, *Who We Be: The Colorization of America.* New York: St. Martin's Press, 2014.

Ta-Nehisi Coates, *Between the World and Me.* New York: Spiegel & Grau, 2015.

Michael Eric Dyson, *The Black Presidency: Barack Obama and the Politics of Race in America.* New York: Houghton Mifflin Harcourt Publishing Company, 2016.

Eddie S. Glaude, *Democracy in Black: How Race Still Enslaves the American Soul.* New York: Crown Publishers, 2016.

Jennifer L. Hochschild, Vesla M. Weaver, and Traci R. Burch, *Creating New Racial Order: How Immigration, Multiracialism, Genomics, and the Young Can Remake Race in America.* Princeton, NJ: Princeton University Press, 2012.

Michael P. Jeffries, *Paint the White House Black: Barack Obama and the Meaning of Race in America.* Redwood City, CA: Stanford University Press, 2013.

Ibram X. Kendi, *Stamped from the Beginning: The Definitive History of Racist Ideas in America.* New York: Nation Books, 2016.

Erika Lee, *The Making of Asian America.* New York: Simon & Schuster, 2015.

Gary May, *Bending Toward Justice: The Voting Rights Act and the Transformation of American Democracy.* New York: Basic Books, 2013.

Barack Obama, *Dreams of My Father.* New York: Three Rivers Press, 1995.

Daria Roithmayr, *Reproducing Racism: How Everyday Choices Lock in White Advantage.* New York: New York University Press, 2014.

Index